BIGFOOT
in Art History

Scott Marlowe

Cover by Peter Loh

First published in the United States by Pangea Press

Pangea Press
514 Winter Terrace
Winter Haven, FL
33881

ISBN: 978-1492313687

DEDICATION

To Art-Lovers who are also Bigfoot fans everywhere. This will confirm that the Bipedal Hairy Primate has graced the creative world for centuries and demonstrate that, for all those who enjoy the Creature who are mobility challenged, you don't have to hunt for Bigfoot in the forests, swamps or mountains. You can contribute to our understanding of the Animal in museums and galleries as well.

Contents

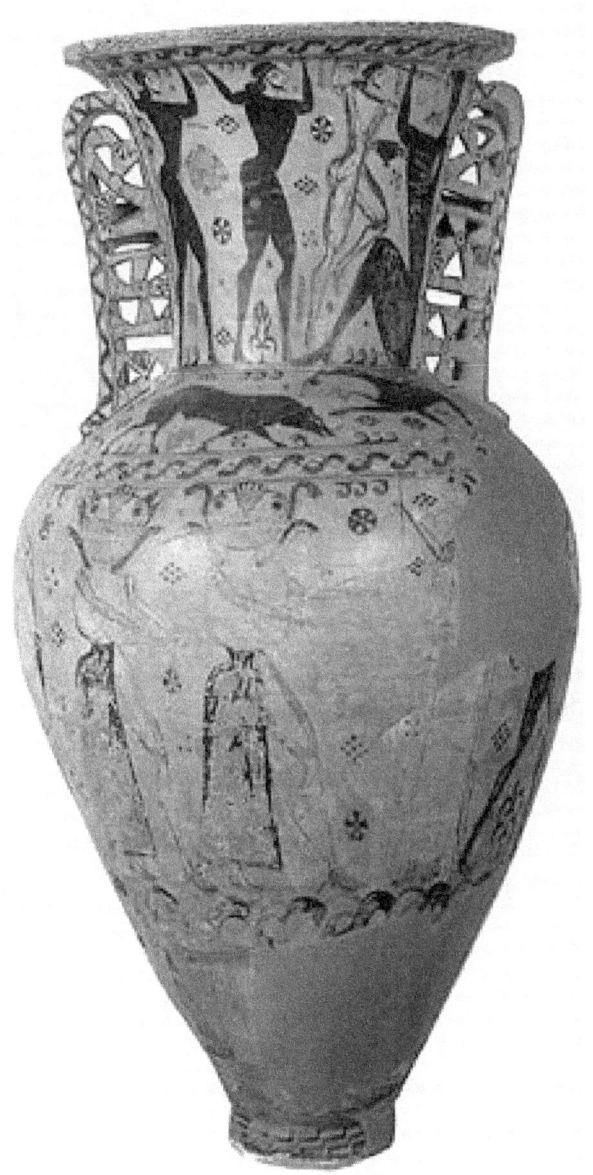

Protoattic amphora by the Polyphemos Painter, 670-660 BCE. Eleusis Museum, Eleusis.

Introduction

The term "Bigfoot" was coined by news media in 1958 to describe a large human-like creature to which a number of large animal tracks found in the Pacific Northwest of the North American Continent were attributed during the middle of the 20th century.

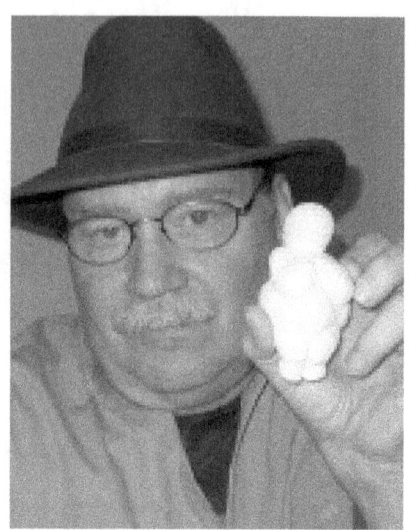

Native American folklore told about a huge forest-dwelling, bipedal, wild man, colloquially named "Sasquatch", "Oh-mah" and "B'gwas", for centuries before the modern terminology was applied to the animal and popularized by the mass media.

In actuality the term "Bigfoot" has come into such common use today that it is now synonymous with nearly all hairy, bipedal, unexplained primates — regardless of their local designations — elsewhere in the world. As a point of fact, there are hundreds of colloquial terms by which this creature is known on all the temperate continents — all of which predate the advent of the modern "Bigfoot" nomenclature

Given this revelation, I became interested in the historical accounts of Bigfoot creatures after researching the local terms used to designate these animals. Realizing that the legends surrounding this wild man would certainly have found representation in artistic expression prior to the development of modern photographic technology I began collecting information for this book.

Typically, the study of art history focuses largely on Indo-European art and begins with the prehistoric artifacts, petroglyphs, pictographs and sculptures found in the cave complexes of Southern Europe and other Paleolithic communities in this region of the globe. There are ample examples of lithic period art incorporating Bigfoot-like animals to be found throughout the world. But, few of these representations are contemporaneous with this European prehistoric era that I have been able to verify thus far in my studies.

However, to truly appreciate the scope of Bigfoot's "modeling career," one must also include aboriginal depictions in America, Australia and Africa, as well as Oriental and Occidental art resources in a comprehensive evaluation of the animal's artistic representation prior to the modern era and its contemporary technologies.

Indeed, the appearance of this animal in artistic expression over nearly the entirety of human artistic and technological history would seem to preclude the notion that the creature's reality is merely one of modern invention, conspiracy, or casual deception and is thus worthy of a examination, if not a serious scholarly study.

Before the skeptics start their moaning, you should expect "Bigfoot" as depicted in art to vary in its physical appearances from culture-to-culture. It will not necessarily have uniform traits such as identical size, form, height, preferred posture, behaviors and so forth. This can complicate our examination of the creature in artistic representation if we let our own cultural conditioning color our expectations of what the animal "has to" look like and how, and in what framework, it should appear. "Culture-Bound Blindness" is the inability to transcend one's own cultural perspective when viewing art.

I'm going to ask you to view the art work presented here and try to put yourself in artist's time, place and circumstance. I'd like you to be open to interpretations of the examples – even if they conflict with your own ideas – and try to consider our discussions as possible explanations for the subject matter within the structure of chronology and situation that apply to the art work being viewed.

Of course, there are alternate (and not so radical) interpretations of the images presented here. However, I would like to point out that the "mainstream" explanations for these images are no more likely than those that I have suggested — given the sometimes abstract nature of art and the fact that we can not ask the artist what he or she intended to portray.

BIGFOOT IN LITHIC ART

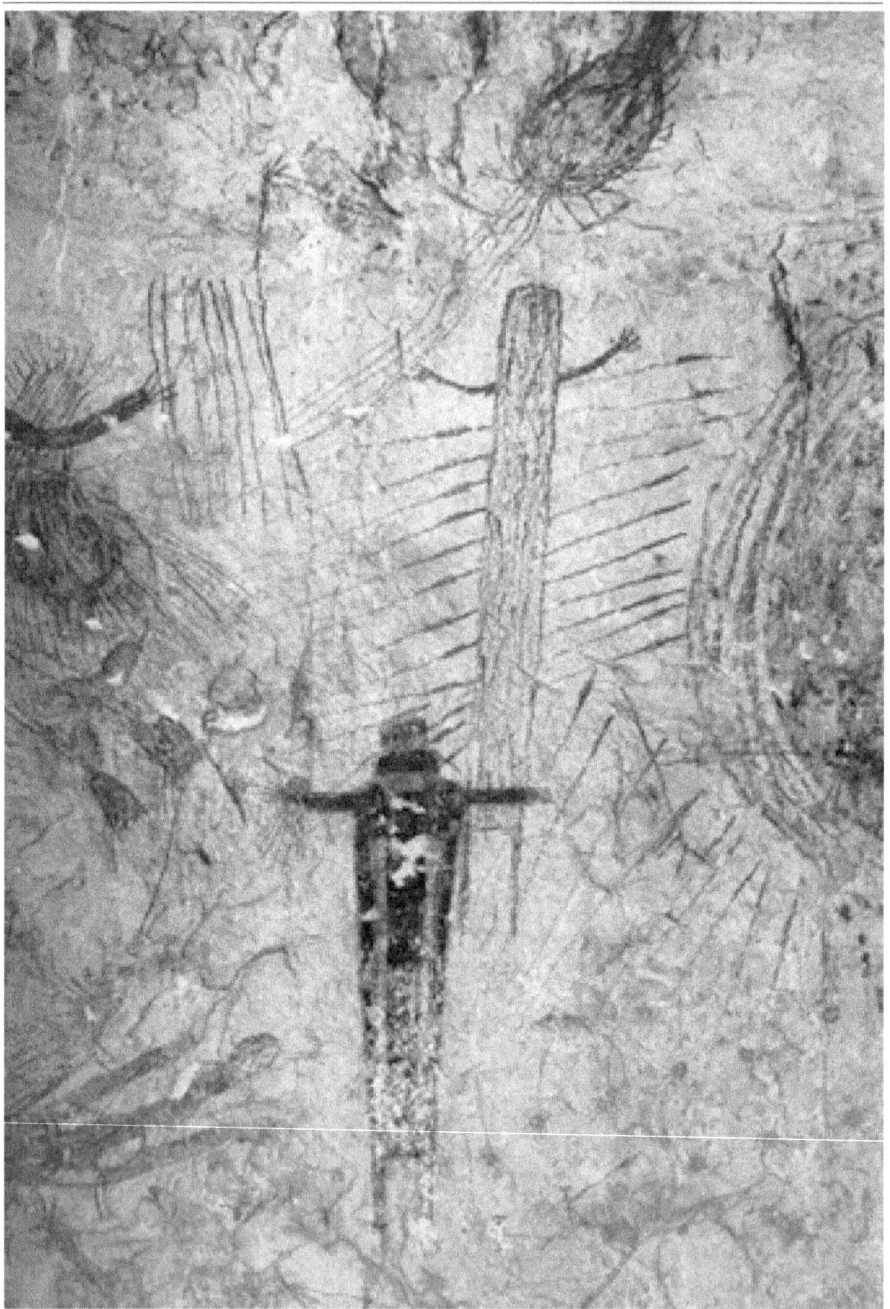

Dated to 4,000 years ago -- about the time the Egyptians were building the Great Pyramid -- Native Americans painted this image in Panther Cave located at Seminole Canyon State Park and Historic Site in Comstock, Western Texas.

Bigfoot in Lithic Period Art

As I previously stated, unknown Bipedal Hairy Primates, or BHPs (perhaps a more generally descriptive acronym for Bigfoot) do not appear in the cave paintings or sculpture of prehistoric Europe to my knowledge -- as of this writing. However, Upper Paleolithic painting, drawing and sculpture that appears to include BHPs did appear in Eurasia, Africa, South America and Australia in the time period spanning 10,000 to 50,000 years ago.

In the Americas, Neolithic art dating From 9000 to 5000 years old also include some depictions of creatures that appear to be Bigfoot — or at least that are Bigfoot-like. Some of one cave paintings that I was able to discover that appear to date from as long as 50,000 years ago.

According to Janson's History of Art (Seventh Edition), "Some scholars suppose that image making and symbolic language as we know it are the result of the new structure of the brain associated with Homo sapiens sapiens. Art emerges at about the same time that fully modern humans moved out of Africa and into Europe, Asia and Australia, encountering – and eventually displacing – the earlier Neanderthals (Homo neanderthalensis) of western Eurasia." Given that Bigfoot is allegedly a closely related primate ape species to modern humans, I would speculate that the lack of abundance of BHPs in art of this period is due to the perception of these creatures as akin to us.

Thus they were seen and depicted as being essentially identical to anatomically modern humans by early artists. Indeed, the perception of BHPs as being "different" from us appears to coincide with the human understanding that also allowed us to differentiate Homo sapiens from our other anthropological relatives through intellectual, anatomical and technological requisites.

Recent genetic studies strongly suggest that the abundance of body hair common to Bigfoot, and known as congenital generalized hypertrichosis in humans, is a condition common to relic hominids. CGH is now an extremely rare genetic disorder characterized by extreme hair growth, typically on the face and upper body. Although unusual in Homo sapiens, (individuals with this genetic "disorder" have appeared in circuses as "dog men" and "ape men" for years) the condition was apparently the status quo for other hominid species.[1]

Therefore, I would further speculate that this obvious visual feature would have formed a basis for early differentiations to be found in representations appearing after the Lithic Period artistic expressions.

In researching this book I found but one website that attempts to delve into the issue of Bigfoot renditions in prehistoric art history.[2]

The writer on this site, Stanislaw Szukalski, admits that he lacks scholarly credentials. So it might be inappropriate to consider his writing as a credible critique of this topic.

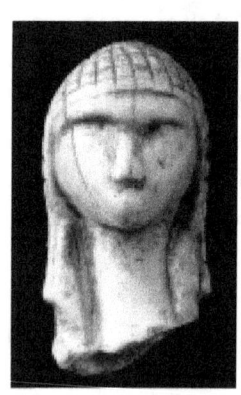

Nevertheless, I would like to begin this discussion with Mr. Szukalski's assertion that the famed ivory carving Dame a la Campuche (see photo left) found in the Musee des Antiquites Nationales, Saint Germain-en-Laye and dated to 22,000 BCE is actually a sculpture of the head of a Bigfoot female and not that of a human.

Personally, I can not distinguish a logical rationale to support the writer's assertion, given the obvious modern human features of the carving,

I would suggest that a closer candidate for a prehistoric sculpture of a Bigfoot female would likely be (and this is equivocal) the Venus of Willendorf (right) dated to 28,000 to 25,000 BCE to be found in the collections of the Naturhistorisches Museum in Vienna, Austria.

This is particularly so in the light of similar carvings recently

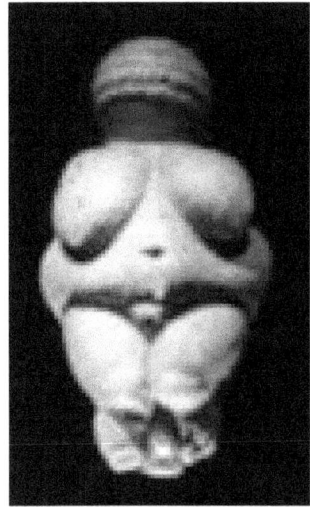 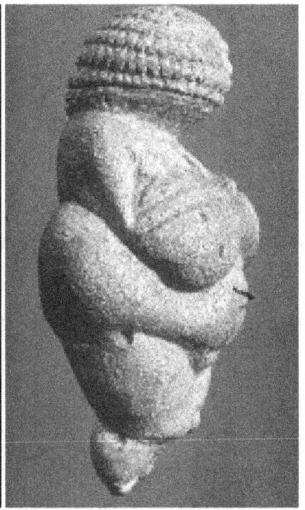 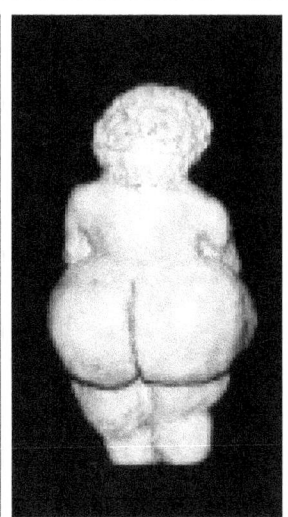

uncovered in Russia. This sculpture has more anatomical features in common with those of a BHP female. However, I am quite dubious (to say the least) of this attribution as to the real-life model for this work of art.

Compare the figurine of the "Venus of Willendorf" to the famous image of "Patty", the female Bigfoot from the well-known Patterson-Gimlin film taken near Bluff Creek, California in the 1960s on this page.

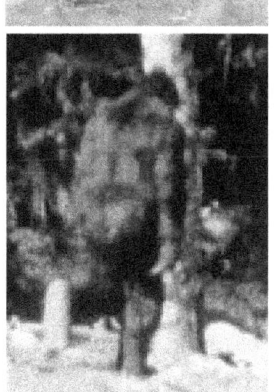

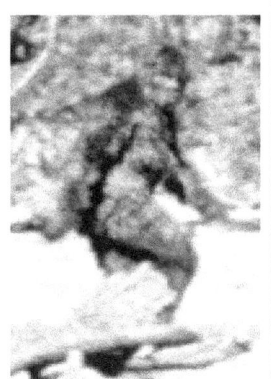

The top images are frontal, side and posterior views of the Venus. Below the posterior view of the Venus appears a posterior view of a gorilla.

Below that are images of the female "Bigfoot" from the Patterson-Gimlin film.

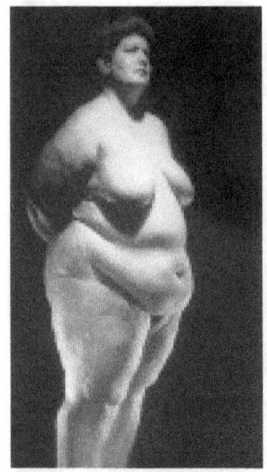

What do you see?

Considerable mammaries and a pronounced posterior as well as a big boned body.

Could these carvings be indicating something more unusual than an obese human female? Take a look at the photo of a mesomorphic female (see photo left) and see what you think.

Except for the apparent coiffure of the Venus figurine, the sculpture could just as easily be a rending of either the gorilla or "Patty." Yet, at least one expert, M.K. Davis, suggests that Patty does indeed have a hairstyle that is visible in clarified images from the Patterson-Gimlin film.

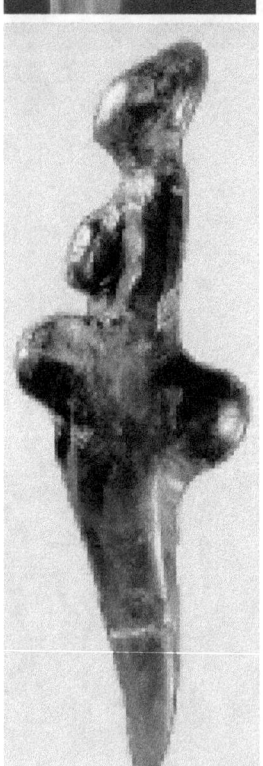

There are many examples of Venus figurines. Some others resemble the Willendorf rendition. Others do not. As an example of a Venus that does not, let's examine a Gravettian Period piece dated to 26,000 years ago from Russia (see photo below left)

It has some of the same hip area characteristics and distended belly as the Willendorf style carvings, but pay close attention to the shape of the head. Is that a beehive hairstyle or does it indicate a sagittal crest found on the cranium of a variety of animals -- including, apparently, a Bigfoot?

The distended belly of the Gravettian piece could also represent a pregnant woman with a transverse fetus in her last trimester.

If this is a "fertility goddess" then why would it take this form?

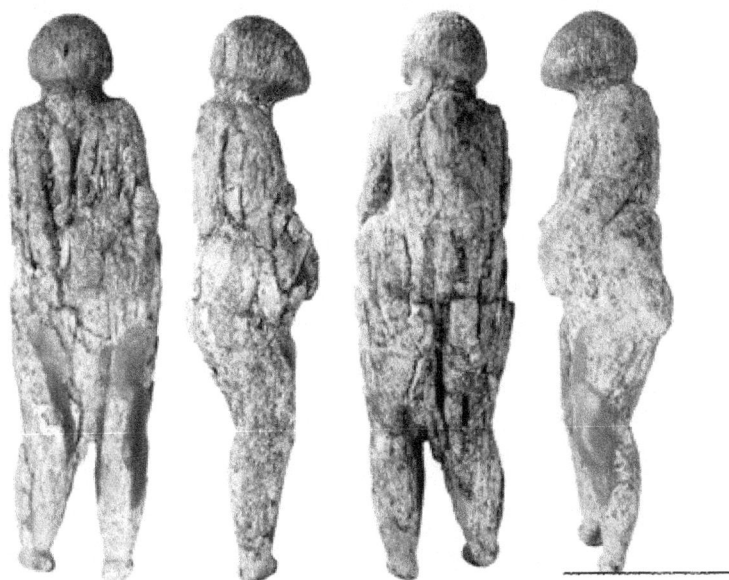

Transverse births are often fatal to both the mother and infant. This form of difficult birth eventually gave rise to the Cesarean delivery method because of the mortality rate.

It's also interesting that a considerable number of female Bigfoot sightings, where a pregnant Bigfoot is reported, note that the animal appeared to be carrying its fetus in this manner. Could infant and maternal birth mortality be a reason that the animal is so rare?

The Venus pictured above is from the Upper Paleolithic (roughly 10,000-40,000 years ago). This is the period during which humans expanded "tool-making" to include art and adornment.

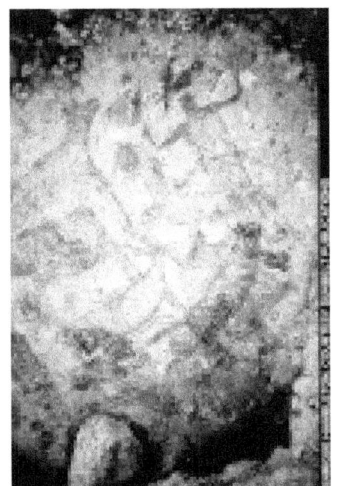

Fig. 1 - *A Cave Painting at El Raton, Baja California. Similar depictions can be found at La Trinidad, Mexico. These are believed to be about 7000 years old. Many of the images have Bigfoot-like features.*

Venus figurines have been discovered in locations ranging from the mountains of Spain to as far east as Siberia. But, the cultural significance of these carvings remains unclear to anthropologists.

Are the figurines really some sort of fertility talisman as the current thinking in archaeology would have us believe – or are they trying to describe something else entirely?

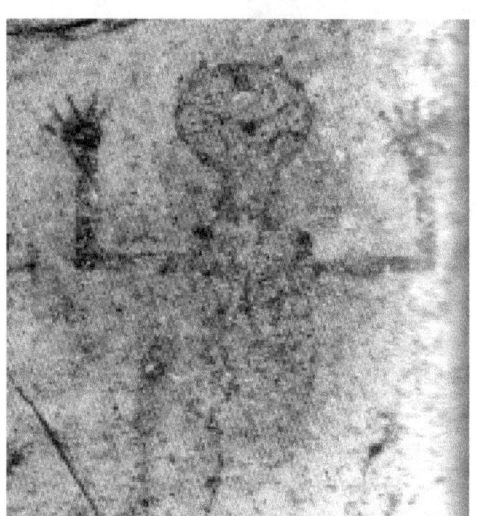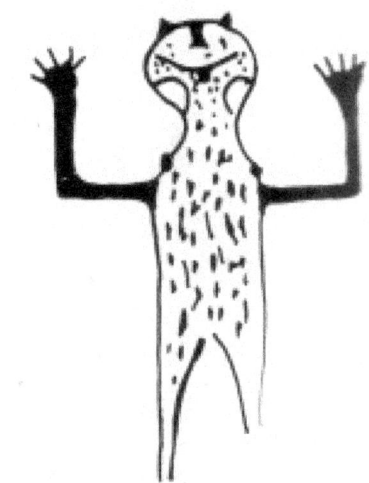

Fig. 2 - *This cave painting can be found in Edmonson County, Ky at a place called the "Asphalt Rock Site," where a group of three Paleolithic rock shelters lie beneath the shadow of cliffs overlooking the Green River.. The detail drawing suggests that this image is not one of a human. The image is thought to be among the older pictographs at the site dating back to 7000 years BCE.*

There are other examples of BHPs in cave art found in many places around the world – particularly in the aboriginal rock paintings of Africa, Australia and in the Americas such as those displayed below and on the following pages.

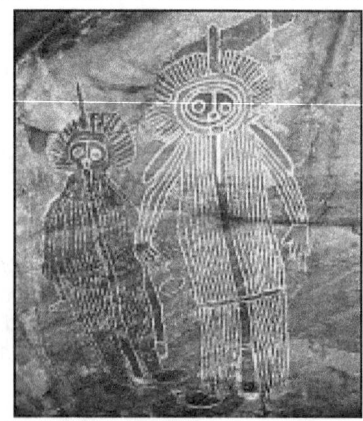

In the Kimberly area of Australia you will find a rock art image of the "Lightning Brothers" (see photo right).

Some people have suggested that the being depicted is wearing a space suit.

But, could the bulk of the body and rays about the head be intended as hair and the "spike" at the center of the cranium be a sagittal crest common with ape species?

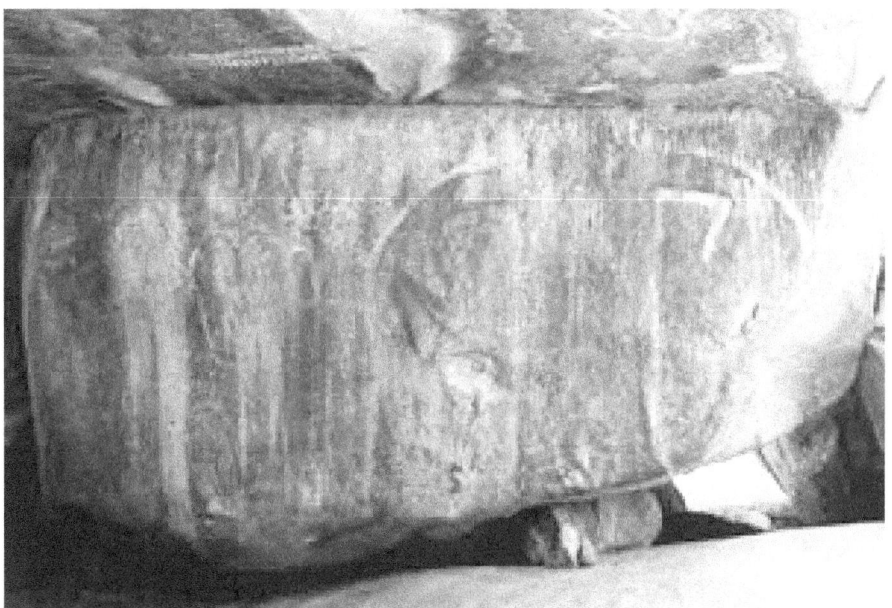

Outside of Porterville, California, located on the Tule Indian reservation, you will find this pictograph (see photo above) of what some claim be a family of Bigfoot. First documented by Mallory in 1889 and again by Stuart in 1929, this pictograph (above) is referred to as "The Hairy Man" or "Hairy Family."

The larger male is drawn at 2.6 meters in height and 1.8 meters wide; the female is shown at 1.8 meters high and 1.2 meters wide; the young "Bigfoot" is 1.2 meters tall and 1 meter wide.

As discussed by Kathy Moskowitz-Strain at the International Bigfoot Symposium held at Willow Creek, California in September of 2003, the unusual shape of the head with vertical lines apparently representing hair and the large feet of the subject, in addition to the

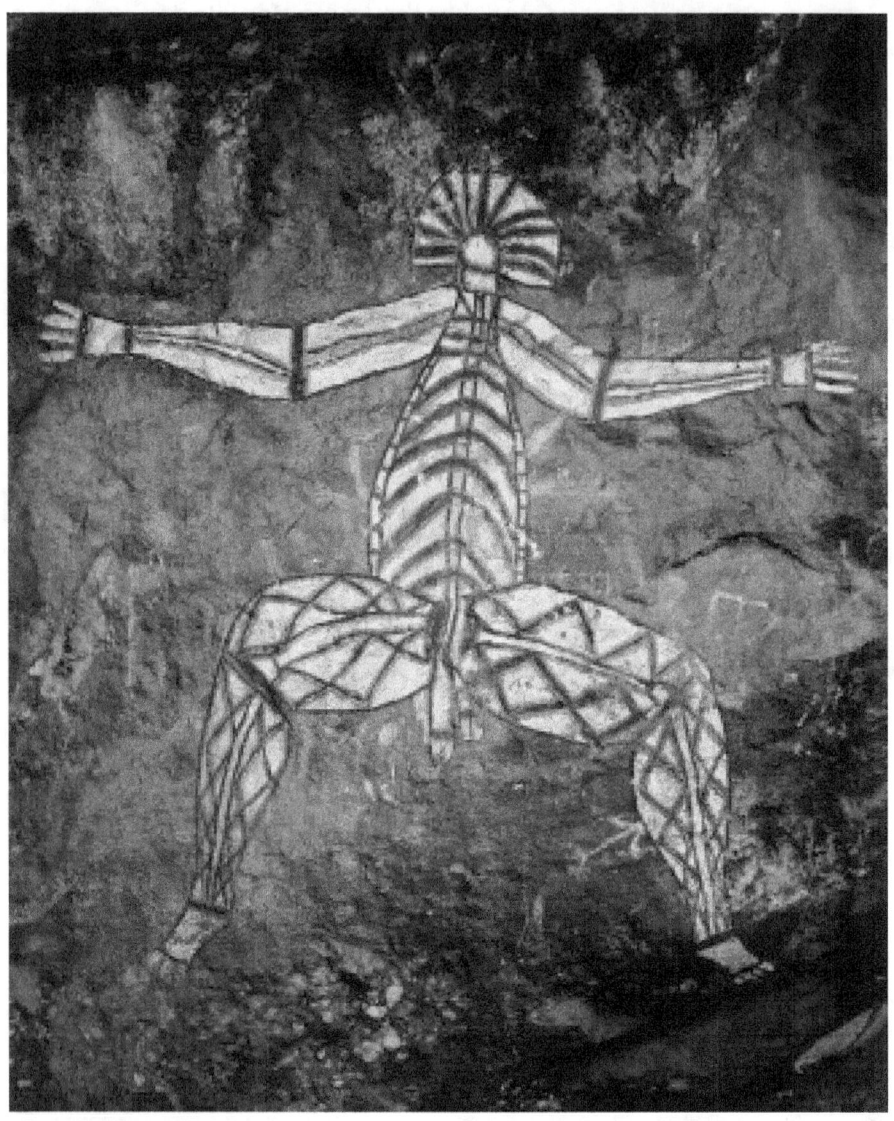

environmental context of the images, suggests that the artist was intending to depict BHPs and not humans in these "Hairy Man" pictographs.

Near of Darwin, Australia is the Kakadu National Park where one can admire magnificent, prehistoric, aboriginal cave paintings, like those pictured here. Scientific dating has placed the origins of the

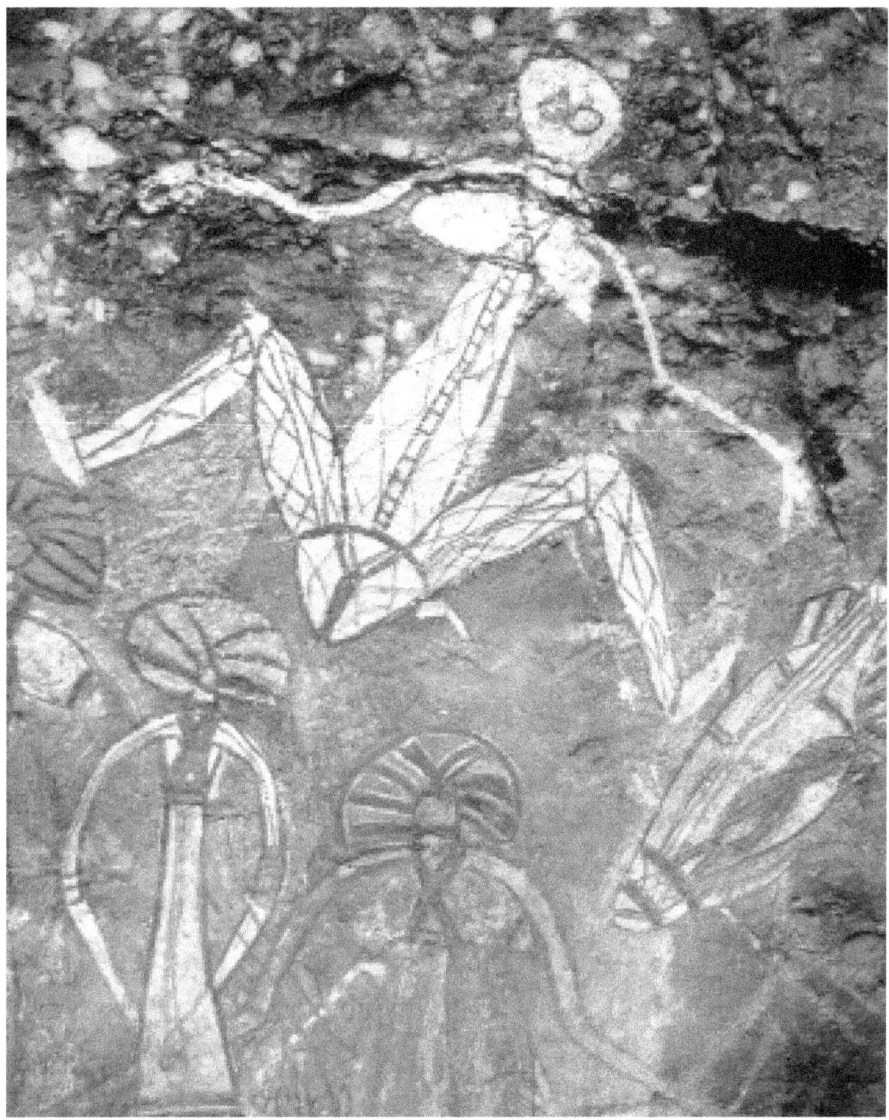

rock art in this area between 25,000 and 50,000 years BCE. Local legend attributes this image to Nabulwinjbulwinj (image on the left prior page), obviously a male - a dangerous spirit who eats women after knocking them out with a thrown yam. In some areas of the world, Bigfoot creatures are said to be cannibalistic and primates often reported to throw rocks and other projecta at those who venture too close to them.

Could the "spirit" of Aboriginal Legend actually be a Yowie — Bigfoot's cousin from down under?

Yet, why would there be the image of a female (image on the right) appear nearby? Is she intended to depict a victim or a mate?

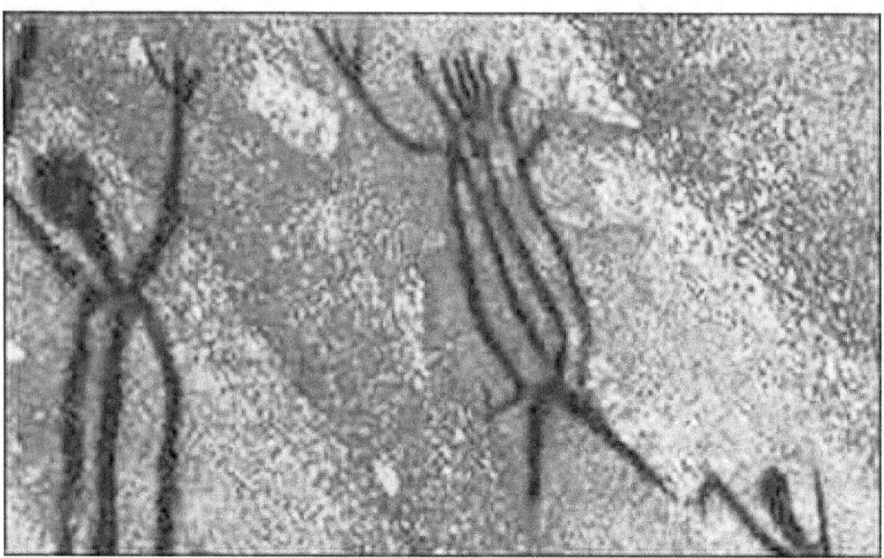

Similar pictographs (see photo above) located in South America imply the same subject matter Stone tools and charcoal from Serra Da Capivara in remote northeast Brazil contain evidence of human habitation beginning about 50,000 years ago.

In this pictograph you will note that humans are drawn with solid round heads and necks while the "creature" in the center is shown with an apparently hairy body and neckless head — features common to eyewitness accounts of Bigfoot sightings also know as the "Mono Rei" or "Mapinguary."

In summary, our quick and limited glimpse of lithic art found around the world, has revealed a number of examples of prehistoric images that seem to resemble Bigfoot-like animals.

Consider "stone-age" man. He has no written language. He (and she) spend most of their time hunting and gathering food resources and shelter materials. They cared for their sick and injured in a tribal society and cooked, crafted clothing, and had to make every "convenience" they needed to live themselves. They may have to migrate distances to provide for themselves and they have families to raise.

There is little time in the day for them to pursue art and artistic expression, yet they managed to find time to do so. Their art is intended to communicate what they observed around them. Like all mammals, humans learn by observing and discerning cause and effect relationships.

The subjects they choose for their expression are things that are important to them. They may be commonplace or fantastic, unusual or out of the ordinary.

What sort of things do you collect when you travel to places that you've never been before? What sights cause you to pull out your camera and take a snapshot? Remember, lithic man didn't have a Polorard or Kodak. Put yourself in their place.

Here, we are not only seeing parts of the world that many of you have never traveled to and becoming part of a culture we've not experienced before. We're looking back in time as well.

At the very least, this inquiry into primitive man's experience should raise a few questions about the casual application of "Occam's Razor" to artistic representations from our own point of view and suggest that a more serious assessment of prehistoric art from other time periods and locations should be undertaken to catalog anomalies that are found in the imagery that is the topic of this study and its underlying premise.

BIGFOOT IN SUMERIAN ART

Bigfoot in Sumerian Art

I had previous postulated that human perception of BHPs as being like unto us was due to the intellectual and technological closeness of Bigfoot to the "primitive" humans of the day. I find some support for my conjecture from the following information.

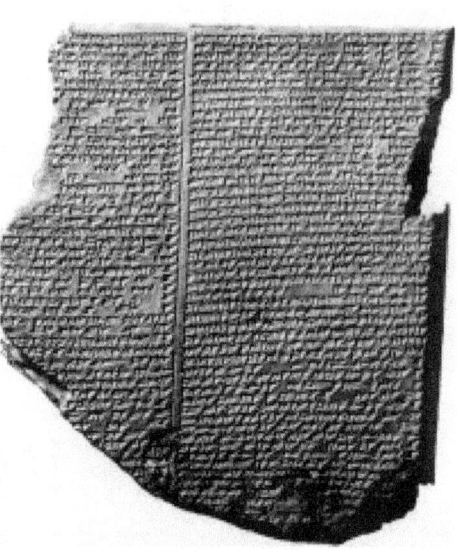

Table 1 of the Gilgamesh saga

The first written mention of a creature that fits the general profile of a Bigfoot creature is found in Tablet 1 of the Epic of Gilgamesh dated to some time between 2750 and 2500 BCE.

The Gilgamesh story is the oldest written document of its kind known. Inscribed on 12 clay tablets in cuneiform script, the Gilgamesh epic chronicles the adventures of a historical King of Uruk in ancient Sumeria.

Considered one of the earliest civilizations, Sumeria was composed of city-states located around the lower Tigris and Euphrates rivers in what is today southern Iraq.

In the epic a character, Enkidu, (some older versions of the epic transliterate Enkidu's name as "Enkimdu", "Eabani" or "Enkita"), is described as a wildman reared by animals. Enkidu's description is strikingly similar to that of Bigfoot animals reported today. In the story, Enkidu is "tamed" by a female courtesan of the court of Gilgamesh named "Shamhat" and becomes a friend of Gilgamesh. Enkidu has adventures with the story's hero until he dies. Here is a translation of the ancient account from Tablet I of the epic:

When Aruru heard this she created within herself the
zikrtt of Anu.
Aruru washed her hands, she pinched off some clay, and
threw it into the wilderness.
In the wildness(?) she created valiant Enkidu,
born of Silence, endowed with strength by Ninurta.
His whole body was shaggy with hair,
he had a full head of hair like a woman,
his locks billowed in profusion like Ashnan.
He knew neither people nor settled living,
but wore a garment like Sumukan.
He ate grasses with the gazelles,
and jostled at the watering hole with the animals;
as with animals, his thirst was slaked with (mere) water.
A notorious trapper came face-to-face with him opposite
the watering hole.
A first, a second, and a third day
he came face-to-face with him opposite the watering hole.
On seeing him the trapper's face went stark with fear,
and he (Enkidu?) and his animals drew back home.
He was rigid with fear; though stock-still
his heart pounded and his face drained of color.

To summarize the story, Enkidu, was raised by and among animals and seduced into joining the civilized world by a human female. He retained many of his undomesticated characteristics and lived with a hunter prior to migrating to the city to meet Gilgamesh, the king.

Enkidu is just about the physical equal of Gilgamesh and dares to aspire to be the king's rival. Instead, he becomes Gilgamesh's unlikely soul-mate. But, Enkidu meets his demise when the gods punish the duo by inflicting Enkidu with a slow, painful and demeaning death for killing the demon Humbaba and the Bull of Heaven.

Given the significance of Enkidu within the Gilgamesh epic, it was obvious that the character would be depicted subsequent to his appearance in the saga within the art of the period.

Indeed this is the case. There are a considerable number of sculptures of Enkidu without a hairy body dated to around 2500 BCE and among the collections of the Bagdad Museum in modern-day Iraq.

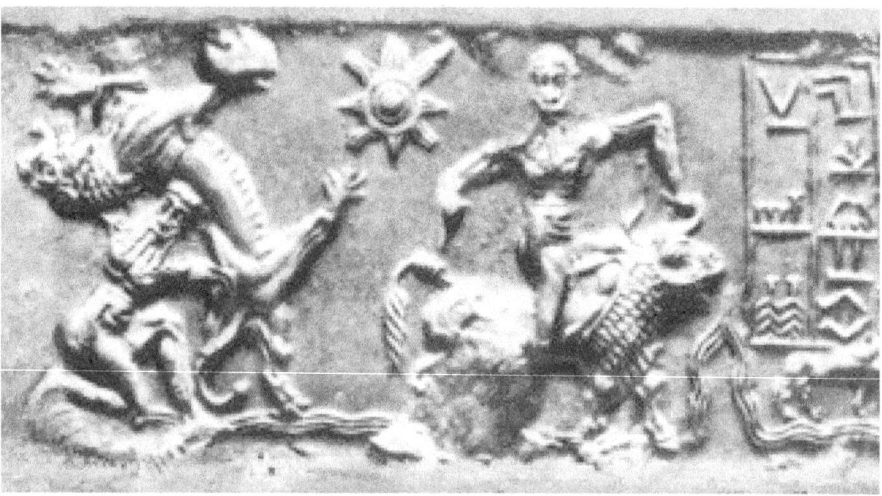

Fig. 3 - *A cylendar seal showing Gilgamesh wrestling a lion (left) and Enkidu (in a more simian depiction) tackling a bull. Many accounts of Bigfoot sightings are also associated with bovines — even today.*

I have selected a few additional artworks here which depict events from the epic adventures of Gilgamesh and Enkidu.

On the bottom of the previous page is an illustration taken from a cylinder seal in which Gilgamesh and Enkidu kill the Bull of Heaven, sent by Ishtar after her marriage proposal was turned down by Gilgamesh. The reader should note that battles with bulls are a common element in Greek hero legends, notably Hercules and Theseus as well as those of Persia and Crete.

Sumeria eventually fell to the Babylonians who incorporated many of the Sumerian heroes into the legends of the new rulers of ancient Persia.

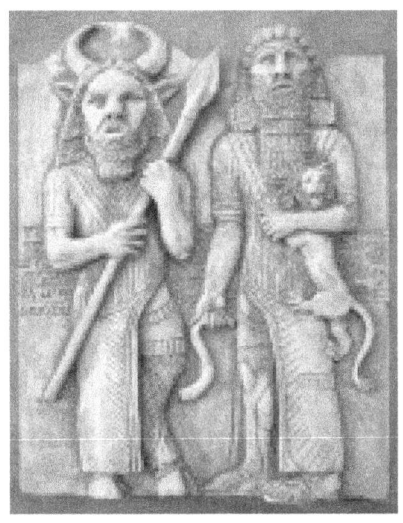

Fig. 4 - *In this bas relief, Enkidu (left) is depicted with horns. This rendition appears to have been picks up by the later Greeks and Romans in the form of the Satyr or Faun. In some artworks Enkidu appears with a horned helmet akin to that of a Viking.*

Relatives of the Enkidu character found in the Epic of Gilgamesh may live on today in the form of the Almasty (Almas) of the Caucasus Mountain region of what is today northern Iran or the Barmanou (or Barmanu) a BHP said to be living in the mountainous region of Afghanistan and Pakistan.

Around 1988, Jordi Magraner, a Spanish national, undertook to methodically research the Barmanou legends of the Hindu Kouch district of Chitral, in the north of Pakistan, and Afghanistan. Unfortunately, Magraner was assassinated in Pakistan in 2002 before his work could be completed.[3]

Notwithstanding this loss and a clear connection to the Barmanu, and unlike the BHP renditions of prehistoric art, there can be no doubt that Enkidu was indeed a Bigfoot creature. While most of the artistic representations of Enkidu in this period are not hirsute, it is clear that he "retains many of his undomesticated characteristics" detailed in the saga.

The failure of artists of the period to illustrate Enkidu as a hairy hominid may be due, at least in part, to respect for their hero (Gilgamesh) who they would not likely want to attribute the same animalistic traits.

However, it's interesting that the normal humans in the story do not see Enkidu as an outcast due to his hirsute appearance. They actually seem to accept him as merely another human like themselves.

This may actually be factual. If you accept that Bigfoot is a form of relic human (and not an undiscovered animal) or that the "monster" is simply afflicted by Hypertrichosis, which is a fairly common genetic human disorder in certain areas of the world. The Sumarians may have been appropriate in their treatment of Enkidu (in today's politically correct sense) both artistically and in fact.

Indeed, the majority population of Georgians, Greeks, Turks and Southern Italians tend to be significantly hairy: While the Portuguese, Spanish, Northern and

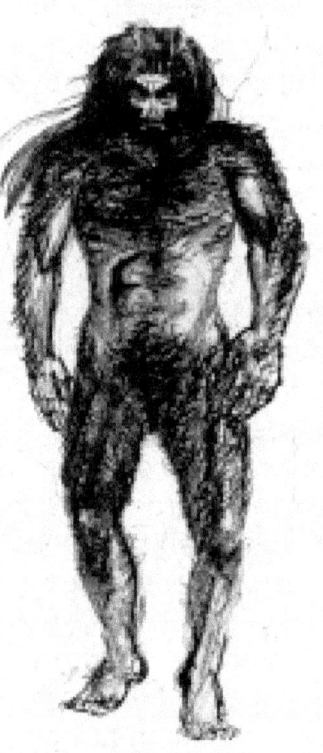

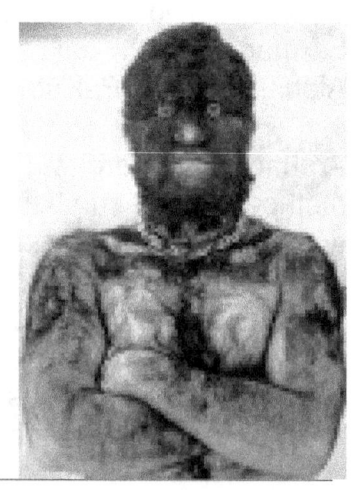

The Barmanu (above) and a photo of a man with hypertrichosis (below). Could this indicate that Bigfoot is actually human?

Central Italians, French, Croatians/Serbs Romanians, Bulgarians, Hungarians tend to be moderately so.

The reader should remember this information as it may be at issue when we take a look at the art from thse regions of the world.

BIGFOOT IN EGYPTIAN ART

Bigfoot in Egyptian Art

Baboons and monkeys are common characters and play a significant and sometimes mysterious role in the religion and in the everyday life of ancient Egypt. This, at first, seems odd as there are not any native apes, monkeys or baboons in Egypt — now or during ancient times.

However, it is clear that the early Egyptians of the Bronze Age (4000 BCE) were well-acquainted with monkeys and often contentious baboons. Indeed, these animals were quite frequently mummified and interred in Egyptian tombs representing the god Thoth or Hapy.

So, I was at first somewhat confounded by the practice of ancient Egyptian artists to anthropomorphize the images of their deities (See the Pantheon of Major Egyptian Gods and Goddesses on the next page).

Thoth, the ibis-headed god of wisdom and learning, was believed to be able to transmute himself and appear in the form of a baboon when he so desired. While the baboon headed-god Hapy (sometimes spelled "Hapi"), the guardian of the lungs, is a constant cover subject for canopic jars which hold the preserved remains of that body organ (see image right at the lower left).

Unlike the Greeks and Romans who came after them and had a fairly consistent pantheon of gods, the Egyptian gods came and went -- depending upon the year and geographical location in Egypt. Some gods were associated with the Upper Kingdom others were venerated in the Lower Kingdom. Some gods were favored by specific pharaohs or their dynasties,

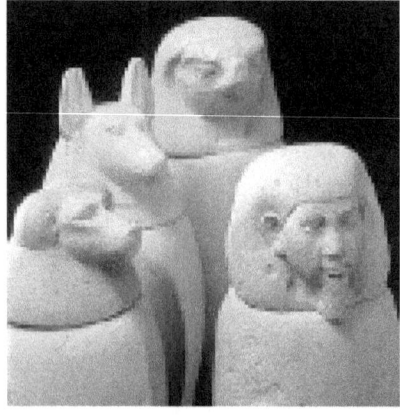

Pantheon of Egyptian Gods and Goddesses

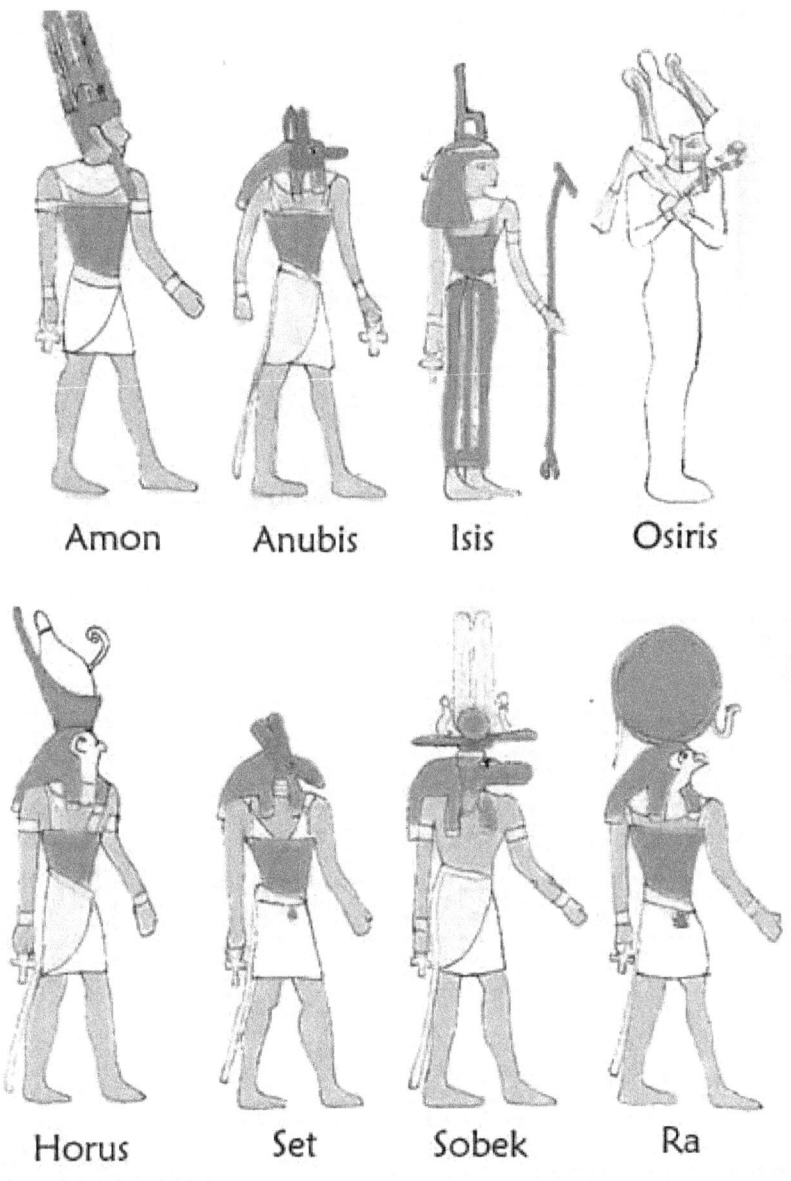

Amon   Anubis   Isis   Osiris

Horus   Set   Sobek   Ra

Pantheon of Egyptian Gods and Goddesses (Continued)

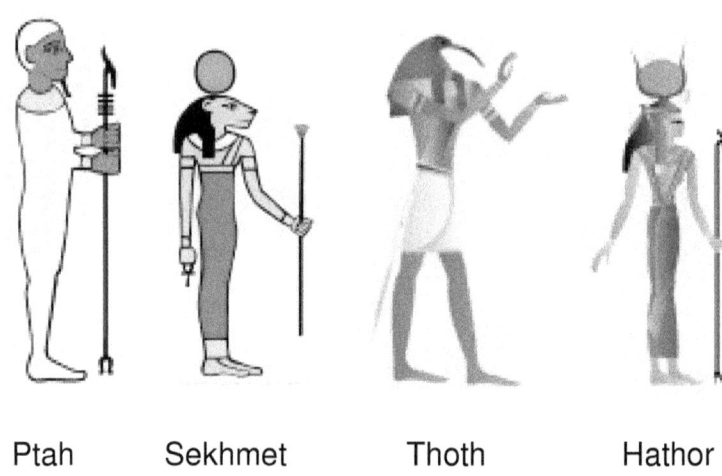

| Ptah | Sekhmet | Thoth | Hathor |

or cities. New gods replaced older gods, and vice versa constantly. But, the Egyptian gods of the Nile delta, likely because of the trade relations with neighboring countries, assimilated foreign gods of the Sinai desert having similar characteristics. On the other hand, the Egyptians were not to proud to adopt the gods of other nations and peoples with whom they communed.

So, at first there seemed to be a lack of a BHP-like characters in ancient Egyptian art that appeared as an obvious primate that was clearly a Bigfoot-like animal. That was until I recalled that not all BHPs are of the giant statue — or even mere human height — which is a common modern misconception.

Some BHPs known around the world are diminutive creatures standing one meter tall or less such as the "Ebu Gogo" of Southern Asia, the "Tokoloshe" (see illustration right) of central Africa or the "Ufiti" of today's Malawi — among others on the African continent.

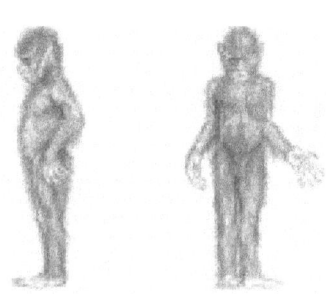

So my attention turned to the one god in the Egyptian pantheon, Bes (or Bess or Bisu), that is an obvious candidate for the attribution as a diminutive Egyptian Bigfoot. To the ancient Egyptians, Bes was the god of luck and probability, a patron of art, music, childbirth, and protector of children. Evolving over time, Bes also became the god of war, a strangler of antelopes, bears, lions, and serpents (this behavior should sound familiar to Bigfoot enthusiasts).

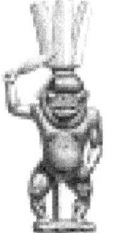

Bes is typically depicted as a hairy, short, nude midget with bug eyes and drooling tongue that is often stuck out. He is also shown with an unusually large head and flat, gorilla-like nose.

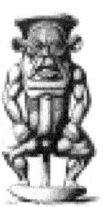

Unlike the other Egyptian gods, Bes is almost always shown in full frontal view instead of i profile (see illustrations on the left) — a depiction that suggests that he is somehow unique among the Egyptian deities despite the "conventional" parentage thrust upon him by the Egyptians.

Some scholars assert that Bes was "borrowed" by the Egyptians and most likely of Nubian origin. Other experts suggest that Bes hailed from the Great Lakes Region of Africa — putting his origins in the Congo or nearby locations. The latter speculation would place Bes' origin in an area from which many Bigfoot-like animal legends of diminutive dimensions are common today; having their roots in oral legends handed down over the millennia.

The designation "Bes" appears to be derived from the Nubian word for "cat" (besa) which literally means "protector.", and indeed, his first appearances in Egyptian art suggest the face of a lion and his body appearing something like that of a crouching cat.

Egyptians routinely kept cats in order to ward off snakes, and creatures that might damage crop resources, such as rodents. Thus, Bes was naturally singled out as worthy of worship in Egypt. Bes' character traits are akin to midget BHP legends from Africa,

Asia and South America and even extend to other "trickster" creatures (we will later examine) found in Europe during post-Egyptian era time periods.

As was the case with many of the Egyptian gods, the worship of Bes was exported to other Mediterranean cultures. Bes was particularly popular with the Phoenicians and the Minoans of Crete and is generally equated with the Greek god Pan.

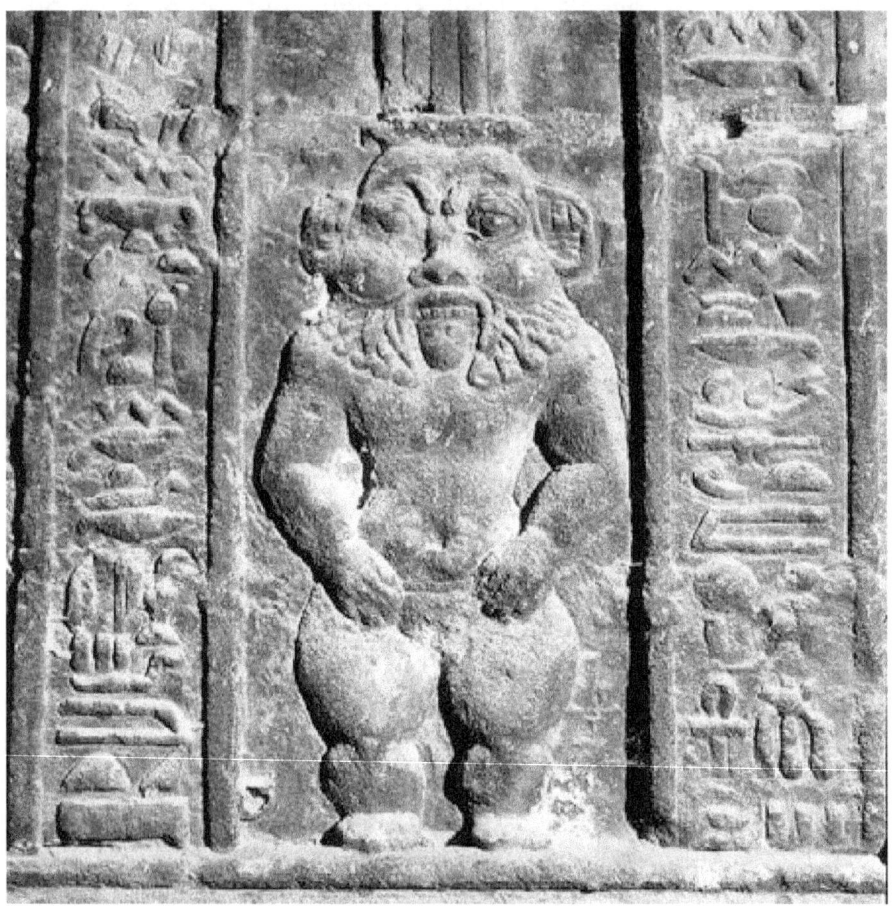

Fig. 5 - *Bes as depicted on a bas relief at the Dendera Temple, dedicated to Bes and the goddess Hathor, Egypt*

Unlike other Egyptian gods, Bes did not immediately disappear from the memory of the populace with the advent of Christian worship.; Legends of a wicked "demon" known as "Bes " was exorcized by Moses because god was terrorizing the neighborhood.

So, we again find that there exists what is apparently a BHP in the art history of the greatest of Earth's early civilizations.

Moreover, the artistic expression of the creature begins to take on the visual characteristics common to a bipedal, hairy, primate — albeit without the conventional physical stature of the typical Bigfoot.

BIGFOOT IN SOUTHEASTERN MEDITERRANEAN ART

Bigfoot in Southeastern Mediterranean Art

It has already been established that the worship of the Egyptian god, Bes, was adopted — probably by Phoenician traders who, through their patronage, spread the worship of this deity throughout the Southern Mediterranean to Carthage and the Minoans living Crete.

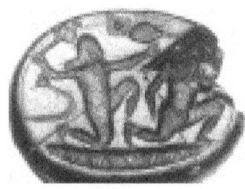 We should note that, over the extensive time line of Egyptian history, the manifestation of Bes evolved from that of a "country boy" to household protector, then to a "party animal" and finally to that of a combatant as depicted on the amulet on the left from Carthage. In the Old Kingdom, Bes was connected with fertility, circumcision and various harvest rituals that, to a degree, reflected the "natural man" aspects of Enkidu. By the Middle Kingdom, Bes began to be regarded as the guardian of the home, children, mothers and a protector of pregnant women.

As the worship of Bes evolved over time his depiction as a dwarf became more common and he was occasionally shown with drums, a tambourine, or playing the flute and dancing in a context connection with joy, lust, wine, and the general pursuit of pleasure.

But, by the Greco-Roman Period in Egypt, Bes had developed into a more menacing figure, and was often depicted with knives and swords. His status as a guardian took a new direction as a defender in man's constant warfare against wickedness.

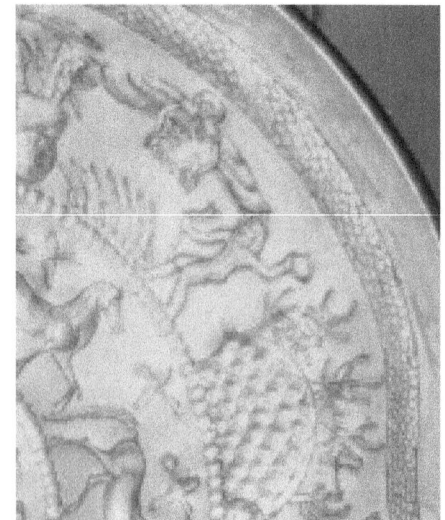

In the different cultures that were exposed to the god Bes, the

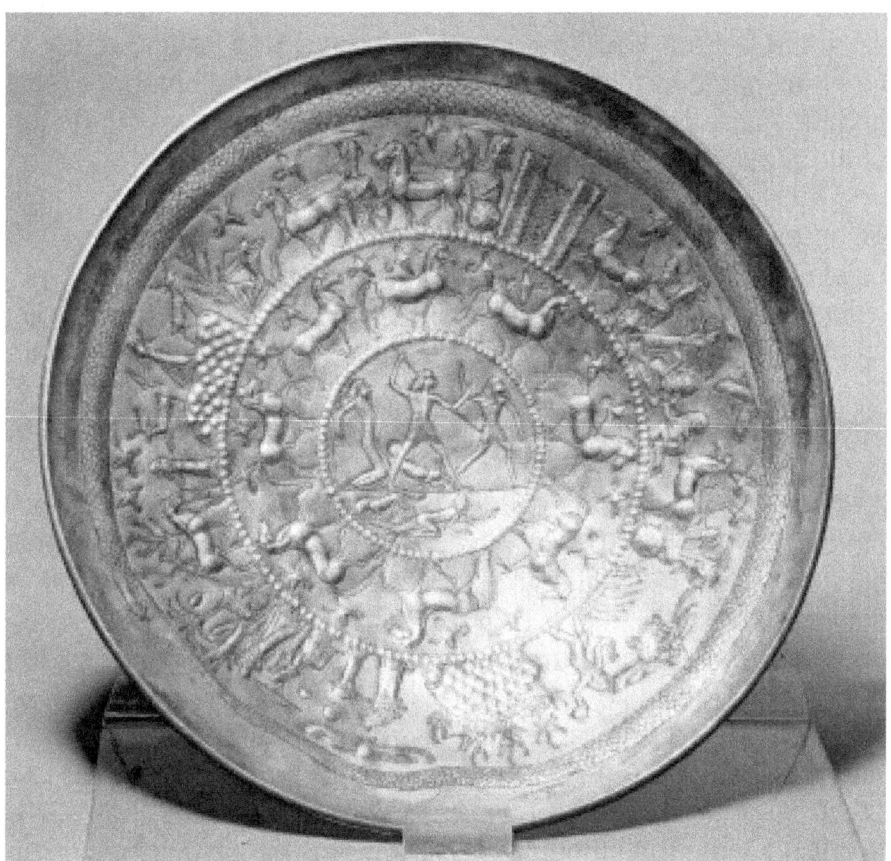

Fig. 6 - *Canciani, F. and Von Hase, F.W. 1979. Bowl, Found at the Grave of Bernardini at Palestrina. c. 2nd century BCE Rome: National Council of Antiquities (or Historical) Research. The BHP is located lower right.*

character of the incarnation changed in accordance with that of the local customs and folklore. By this time, the BHP basis for Bes gave rise to depictions with the bestial appearance of a Bigfoot As in the detail on the lower right of the previous page from the plate illustration above. The human ability to discern the differences between BHPs and people had developed to the degree that artists of the day had little difficulty in rendering BHPs quite differently than they had in the prehistoric and Sumerian periods.

Study the center of the Phoenician plate on the lower right of page 42 at the bottom You'll be able to discern a Bes getting ready to throw a wine cup at someone outside of the detail image. (You'll find the entire plate with the complete scene in context on the top of the previous page).

This "defender" is one of several similar images appearing on that bowl made in Crete around the 2nd century BCE. The bowl was discovered amongst a cache of artifacts in the tomb of Bernardini located at the Roman Villa de Palestrina, a Roman country estate near the site of Praeneste, a town founded circa 800 BCE and first destroyed and later rebuilt by the Romans in the 1st century BCE.

The reader should take particular notice of the low forehead, extension of the jaw, lack of a neck, the nose, especially its deeply sunken bridge in addition to the extent of knee flexing, as well as the obviously hairy body of the BHP which also appears to be holding a tree or vine branch in his right hand (the cup is in the left hand). These "classic" poses and props become more common as the depiction of Bigfoot in art evolved around the Mediterranean and in Europe.

You'll also note the semblance of Egyptian clothed persons at the center of the plate with chariots and combatants in the embossings around the center. The people that are the target of the BHP throwing the wine cup are apparently beating down two additional BHPs.

Of additional interest is that I have located another silver plate, apparently from the same workshop and time period, among the collections in the Metropolitan Museum in New York. However, this artifact is badly eroded and not in the pristine condition of Figure 9.

So, we can conclude from this duplication that the image here is not an anomaly or just a badly crafted item, but rather a repetitive theme thus indicating the popularity of Bes worship in the ancient Southeastern Mediterranean.

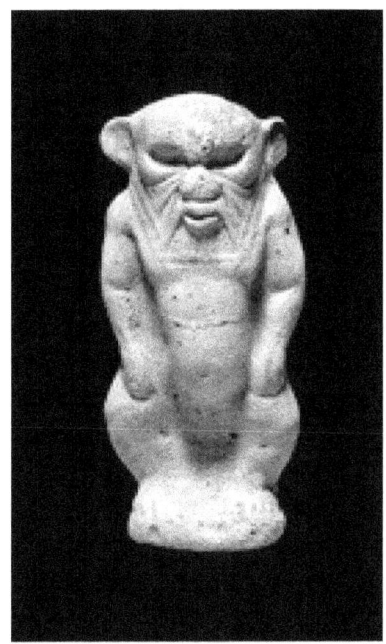

Fig. 7 - On the right is a Bes amulet excavated in Carthage now in the collection of the British Museum in London.

Fig. 8 - In the image below, Bes is featured as a character in the center (lower) of a piece of jewelry that can be found among the collections at the Louve in Paris.

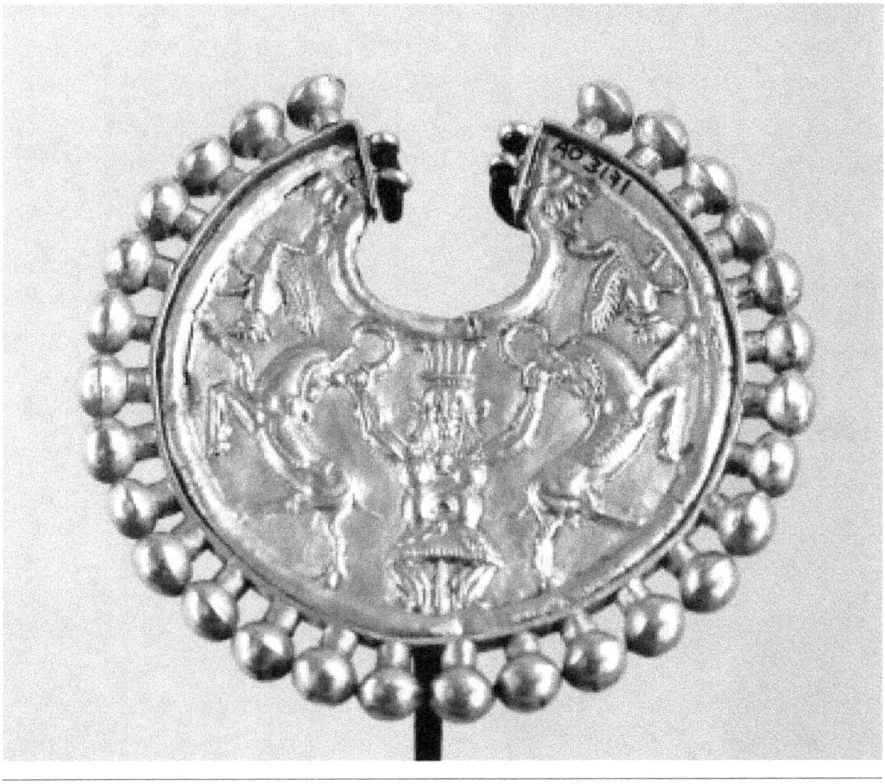

BIGFOOT IN GREEK ART

Bigfoot in Greek Art

While some Southeastern Mediterranean cultures chose to portray the Egyptian god Bes in a more aggressive role conforming to their social character, the Greeks valued Bes' more frivolous side and eventually cast him in the role of their god Pan, a god of nature and the patron of shepherds and their flocks. Indeed, the etymology of the word "Pan" can be traced to the Greek term for "pasture".

Typically, Pan is shown with the hindquarters, legs, and horns of a goat in the same way as the mythical satyr or faun (a young satyr) — but this is not always the case. In the illustration on the right, taken from a Greek vase, Pan is depicted with a more humanlike lower body and the classic pointed ears attributed to this BHP by the ancient Greeks.

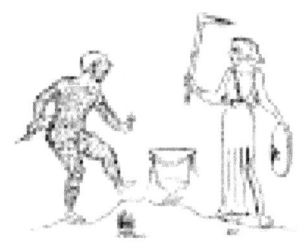

In many scenes appearing on ceramics of the period and in some sculptural works, Pan is usually represented as a seducer of women — a role that well suits the ancient Greek attitude towards the female gender as inferior to men. Some legends of the period trace Pan's parentage to the chief god of the Greeks, Zeus, who could arguably be considered the premier sexual predator in the Greek pantheon. However, some Greek legends hold that Pan was the son of Hermes and a nymph.

Pan has his origins with the Sumerian, Enkidu, and the Greeks , with their typical male dominated romanticism, turned the Story around making their central character the aggressor and blended his nature with that of the Egyptian god Bes.

According to legend, when Pan was first born, those who saw the ugly infant ran from him in terror — thus, the origin of the word "panic." As previously mentioned, satyr creatures were not always depicted as having cloven feet. But, despite his loathsome appearance, Pan again became associated with music (shown often with a "pan flute"), inspiration and sexuality as his tenure in Greek culture evolved.

In another example of this, I submit the drinking cup (right) from a private collection. The era in which this vessel was made was during the time of Philip of Macedonia (Philip II - Father of Alexander the Great) and his more famous son. The conquest of the Persian Empire lead to a period of unification wherein there was a "blending" of Greek and Persian cultures called the "Orientalizing Period.".

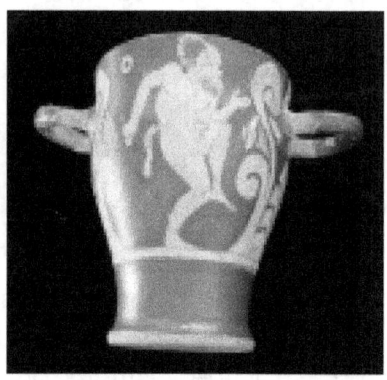

Fig. 9 - *This Gnatha Skyphos, a large cup, is typical of pottery produced in Magna Graecia between 350 to 300 BCE*

Even before this era, Greek artists had been employed by Persian rulers to produce artwork, particularly sculptures and reliefs (owing to their well-known skill), for palaces and public works projects. So, we would expect to see the assimilation of subjects, elements and motifs into Greek art and vice versa.

Now, the ancient Greeks would vehemently deny that they "borrowed" any of their cultural heritage or ideas from other civilizations, as they proudly held that their concepts were original to them. However, we have already seen that the worship of the Egyptian god, Bes, was indeed a "foreign import".

Moreover, we can find another manifestation of Bes in the Greek god "Silenus" (sometimes spelled "Seilenos") who was the Greek god of dance — and most especially — the wine press. (See illustration on the top of the next page).

The reader will recall that these "responsibilities" were among those

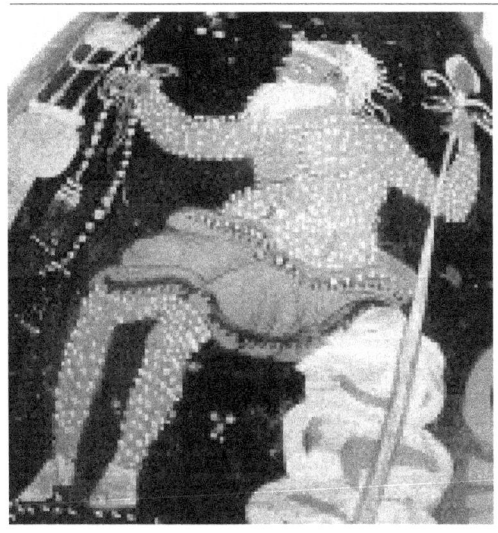

attributed to Bes by the Egyptians.

Silenus often rode in a "sileni" or entourage with the god, Dionysos (Dionysus), appearing as a drunk sitting on the back of a jackass. Represented as a satyr, Silenus (who sprang from the leg of Zeus) was reared in a cave, ostensibly located on the mountain of Nysa, the mythical home of Dionysos and the Okeanid Nymphs.

According to Homer, Mount Nysa was located in Phoenicia near the streams of Aegyptus (other accounts place it in southern Egypt). This setting is, naturally, consistent with that of a Bigfoot (or more correctly put, the Wildman or Almas of Asia) homestead legends arising out of Southwestern Europe and the Near East and infers the aforementioned exchange of cultural ideas. Myth and legend fans will also recognize Silenus as the god who gave the famed King Midas, a ruler of land that became part of the Persian empire, his golden touch.

As the father, grandfather and foster dad of the families of satyrs, fauns and silens, Silenus was usually depicted by artists (see above right) as a carefree, hairy, balding and rotund old man with a snubnose and the ears and tail of an donkey.

An important point here is that cloven-footed, hairy bipeds were not unique to ancient Greece. We have already traced their roots back to Sumeria — which, had become part of the Persian empire. While Pan and Silenus took on a more playful role in Greek BHP folklore, another creature, the giant cyclops, assumed a combative role in Hellenistic culture.

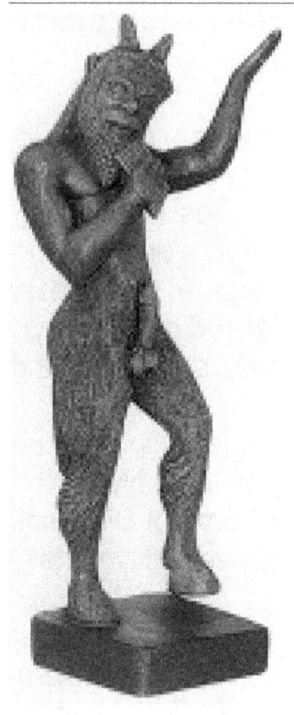

Fig. 10 - *Dancing Pan, From the National Museum, Athens, Greece (500 BCE). This bronze sculpture depicts the god in a more classic manner playing a pan flute and dancing, ready to seduce an unwary female.*

Author Adrienne Mayor, in her book *The First Fossil Hunters*, elaborating on a theory first offered by Austrian paleontologist Othenio Abel, suggests that the inspiration for the cyclops traces to the misidentification of the remains of mammoths found in fossil beds on Crete and in Greece.[4]

This theory asserts that, owing to the large hole found in the middle of the skull where the proboscis was attached, the Greeks mistakenly articulated the massive skeleton and viewed the fossil bones as belonging to a giant, one-eyed, man. However, I'm not sure that this explanation constitutes the entirety of the origin of this legendary creature. I submit that these skeletons may simply have provided a convenient "proof" to the populace that the giants of their legends actually existed.

Some physical characteristics of the cyclops would seem to be exaggerations of traits that are common to a typical Bigfoot — save the attribution of a single eye — which may have been an aggrandizement upon BHP encounter events by eyewitnesses or imparted upon the animal in the retelling of these encounters — as these accounts were passed down orally by storytellers.

It is also possible that there was some confusion in the retelling of these tales of heroic encounters with a cyclops, over time, as the stories usually involved the putting out of an eye which would have left the creature *with* a single eye, assuming that it had been bilocular initially.

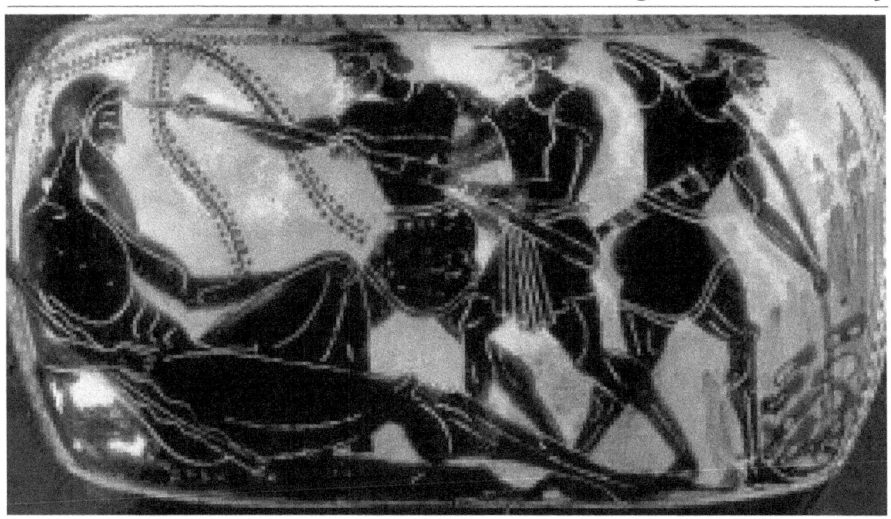

Fig. 11 - *Odysseus and Polyphemos. A black figure ware vase dated to 510 to 490 BCE. Attributed to the painter Theseus. From a collection in the Louvre. Paris, France.*

Fig. 12 - *Paleontologists, Othenio Abel and Adrienne Mayor, speculate that the myth of the cyclops may result from the ancient Greek's discovery of prehistoric juvenile mammoth fossil finds on the island of Crete. The smaller size (relative to those of the adult animals) of these skulls — double-to-triple that of a human skull — combined with the central nasal cavity may have mis-identified as an eye socket, giving rise to the one-eyed giant stories of the region. A mammoth's actual eye sockets are located on either side of the skull — presumably where the ancient Greeks fancied the creature's ear was located.*

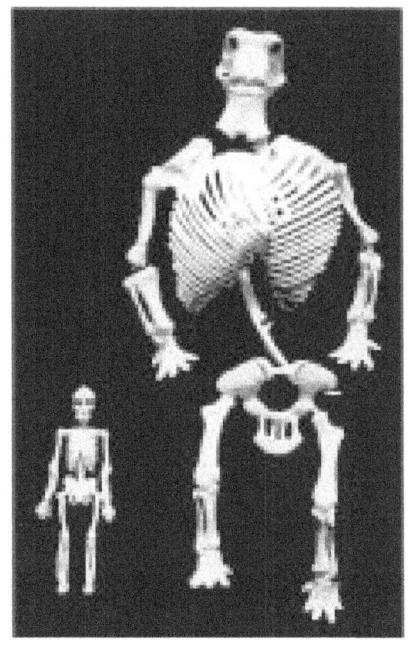

Indeed, the cyclops ceramic appearing on the top of this page may be indicative of this as tales of giant, hairy "monsters" living deep inside the Persian empire (which was later conquered by Alexander the Great) and Crete proliferated throughout the Greek world. (The entire vase appears on page 7. The section appearing here is the upper collar of the vase).

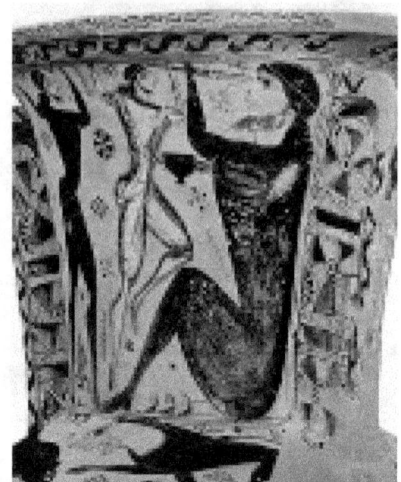

As another example of my thoughts on the mammoth conjecture, I offer the illustration found on a grave marker vase of the period (right).

On the neck of this Orientalizing Period amphora appears the illustration shown, (obviously) taken from the Homeric epic, *The Odyssey*, in which Homer relates the adventures of a crafty Greek hero king on his extended way home from fighting in the Trojan War. The image depicts a scene from the epic where Odysseus blinds the cyclops, Polyphemus, to save his men and himself from becoming a culinary delicacy.

This vase is known to art historians as the "Eleusis Amphora", is dated to early in the seventh century BCE, and suggests the reservations I harbor on this issue. In additional support, I submit that many sculptures produced by the Greek artists of the day featured conventional eye socket anatomy while adding an eye in the center of the creature's forehead.

So, to summarize, the important developments in BHP depictions in ancient Greek art is that while human/animal hybrids (i.e. those with a human torso and head mounted on a grazing animal's body) were considered largely benign, but posing a threat to their women (carrying them off as well as sexually aggressive), while large BHPs became viewed as combatants and monsters.

This new perception of BHP animals as different from humans, and potential competition, sets the stage for the avoidance of these creatures as outcasts by later human civilizations and may even have eventually prompted the persecution of them by man — at least in part resulting in the animal's desire to generally shun direct human contact.

BIGFOOT IN SCYTHIAN ART

Bigfoot in Scythian Art

Scythia, was an area of Eurasia, that extended from the Danube River on the west to the western border of China on the east, south of the Ural Mountains and north of the Black Sea. An area that today comprises much of the Russian steppes and Crimea.

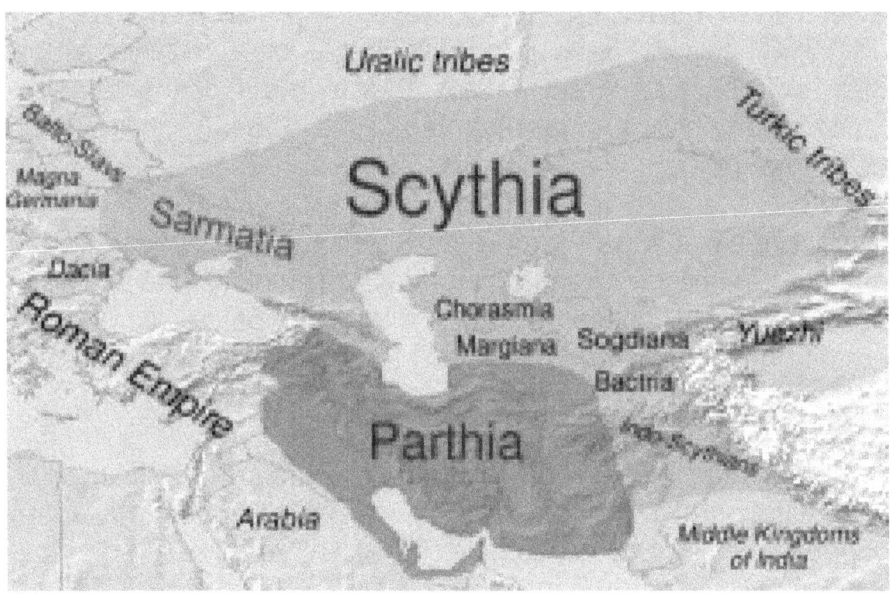

Mount Caucasus where, according to the Greek myth, Prometheus was chained by Zeus after he gave humans the gift of fire, is a mountain within ancient Scythian territory. Scythian lands are also associated with the Greek legend of the Amazon women.

The Scythian empire reached its zenith between the 8th and the 4th century BCE.

Apparently because the Scythians did not have a system of writing, the Greeks considered them to be barbarians. Nevertheless, tombs built for some of the Scythian kings were constructed using the corbelled vault technique identical to that of the famous Mycenaean Greek constructions used for the same purpose. So it is likely that there was some sort of relationship extending back to the

Mycenaeans. Indeed, some Greek legends attribute the initial settling of Scythia to Greek colonists.

The famous French archaeologist, Solomon Reinach, documented striking similarities between Scythian and Minoan-Mycenaean art, particularly in the depiction of animals. "Other motifs of the [Scythian] animal style, too, reappear in Minoan and Mycenaean art. We may cite the animals with hanging legs and those which are curled almost into a circle. Conversely, the standard motif of the Minoan-Mycenaean lion, often represented in the Aegean with reverted head, reappears again in Scythian and Siberian art."

Despite their attitude towards the Scythians, the Greeks traded grain with them for wine and luxury items and employed the Scythians as mercenaries in several of their military campaigns so Minoan and Greek influence in the art of the Scythians was inevitable — if not natural.

The Scythians successfully repelled the Persian king, Darius I in 512 BCE, but it is thought that this war with Darius curtailed an expansion of the Scythian empire.

Scythian's defeated troops sent by Alexander the Great to invade their territory around 325 BCE and retained their independence from Greece.

Reminiscent of the Minoan/ Cretean plate appearing on page 43 in this work is the famous Kelermes Mirror, a section of which appears on the right. Art experts have pointed out elements of Assyrian, Iranian and other artistic styles in the mirror, but I would like to focus on one segment of the piece.

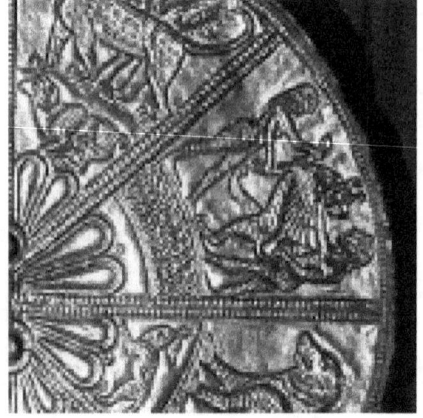

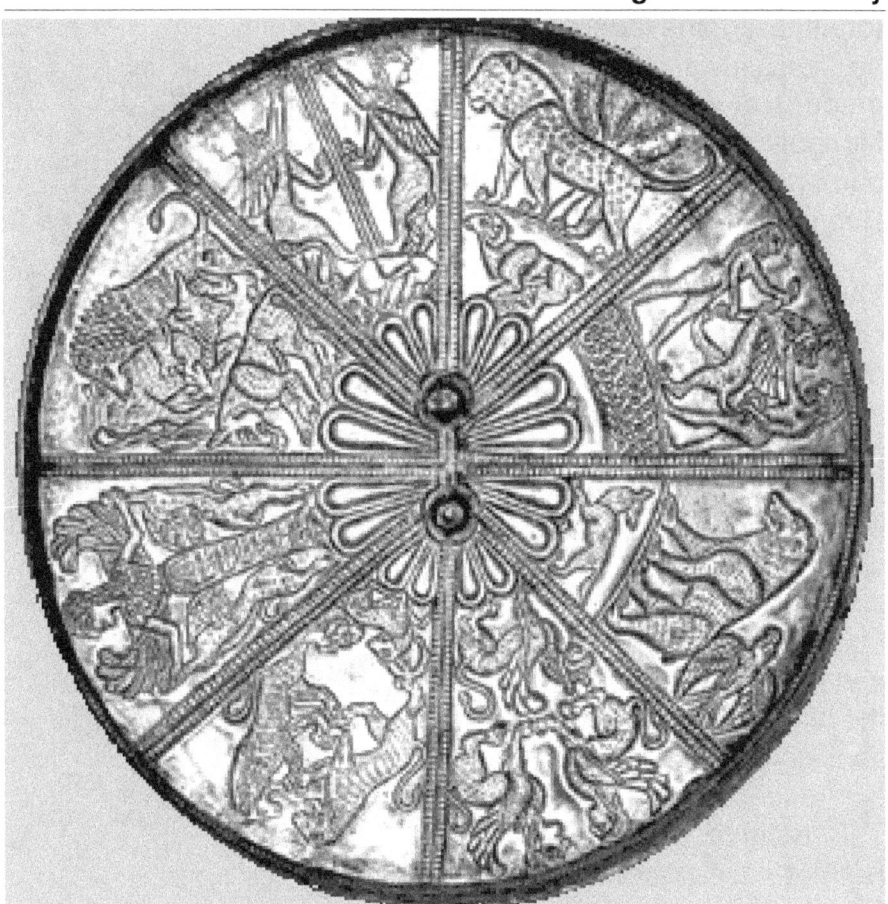

Fig. 13 - *The Kelermes Mirror. circa 620 BCE. Discovered in the Transkuban, near Kelermesskaya Stanitsa. Now among the collections of the Hermitage*

While the "looking glass" side of the mirror is made of polished silver, the gold back of the mirror is comprised of seven equal segments embossed with different characters and scenes from mythology. One section of the metalwork contains images similar to the BHPs we've seen in the aforementioned Cretean metal bowl. These two hairy, bearded men are fighting a winged griffin (see the scene in context with the entire mirror back at 2:00 above).

These bipedal primate figures appear to be depictions of the Almas (or Almasty), the legendary Bigfoot he Caucasus and Pamir Mountains of central Asia. Almas, is the Mongolian word for "wildman", a purported hominid known from the Republic of Georgia to Mongolia.

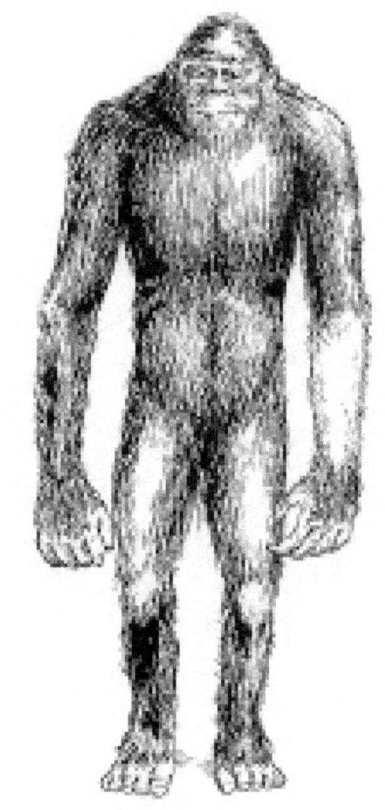

The Almas (see illustration on the right) are said to be human-like bipedal creatures, between five and six and a half feet tall, covered with reddish-brown hair, and facial features that include a pronounced browridge, flat nose, and a weak chin.

Many Russian cryptozoologists assert that there is similarity between the Almas and forensic reconstructions of Neanderthal men.

This believe is shared by some Bigfoot researchers like Stanley Gooch. In his "The Dream Culture Of The Neanderthals" Gooch speculates that a remnant part of the Neanderthal population interbred with Cro-Magnon man leaving fragments of it behind in the form of creatures like the Almas.

However, modern DNA research has all but disproved his conjecture.

Nevertheless, Gooch does bring up some interesting issues and even uses some of the art examples I have presented here, most notably the Cretean Bowl shown on page 43 to support his theory.

We'll speak more about Bigfoot art along the Silk Road Empires later in this book.

BIGFOOT IN ROMAN ART

Bigfoot in Roman Art

According to archaeologists The Etruscans settled in Italy between 900 and 800 BCE. There is still considerable debate about where they originated, but it is suspected that they migrated from the southeastern Mediterranean — most likely from Asia Minor. The Etruscans were a particularly sophisticated civilization and had an alphabet based upon the Greek and also developed their own sculpture and painting style that hints at their cultural origin.

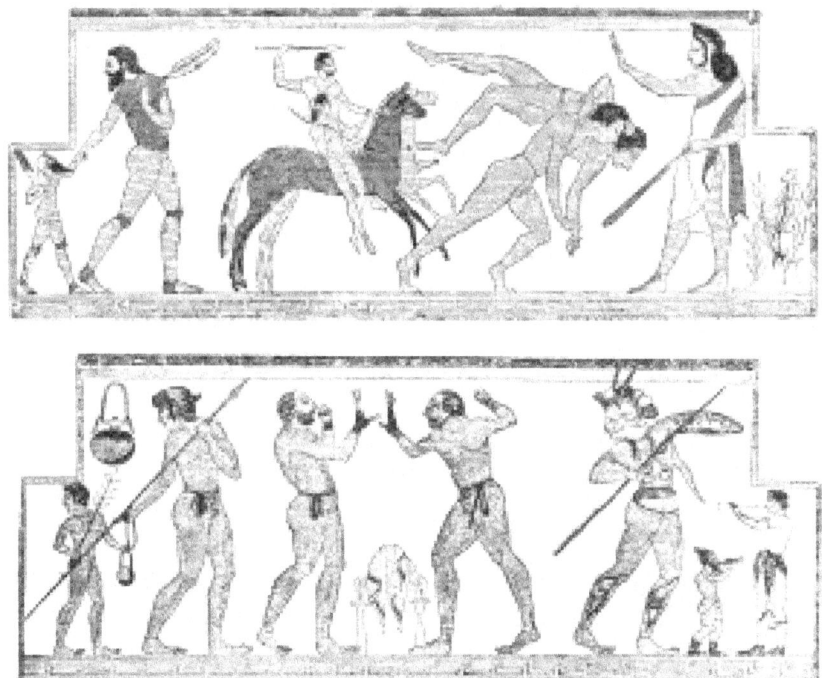

Fig. 14 - *Etruscan dancers and performers. From paintings in the Grotta della Scimia Corneto, circa 500 BCE. Pan in his Etruscan incarnation and his horned companion at the lower right. The BHP appears above them.*

So it isn't surprising that there is a Greek/Crete/Persian "flavor" to Etruscan art and their artistic motifs — including their representations of the pantheon of gods (like Pan and other satyrs and fauns of the lead sileni) — as shown in the fresco excerpt shown below. Take particular note, however, at the image hiding behind the foliage in right side of the upper panel. The image of a BHP concealed among flora here may have been the impetus for an architectural feature that appears later in the Roman era we will talk about later in this section.

Roman art had its origins with the Etruscans, thus they initially absorbed the Etruscan artistic style and Etruscan influence was felt in Roman temple architecture, sculpture, painting and frescos.

But by the beginning of the Roman era, Hellenistic culture had spread to the southern Italian Peninsula and the island of Sicily owing to the Greek colonies located there. After Rome's conquest of Corinth in 146 BCE and later Syracuse, classical Greek art began to exert a greater influence on the austere Romans.

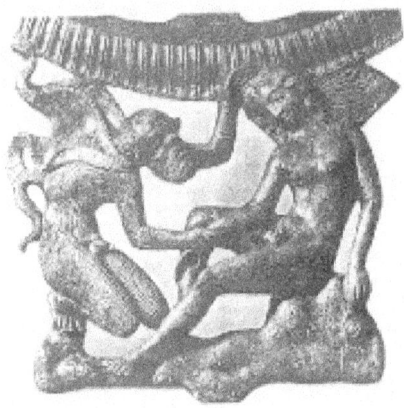

In the later republic and during the early imperial period Hellenistic artists were brought to Rome where they were commissioned to designed buildings, repair older artistic items and create new sculptures. Original Greek art was liberally copied by native Roman artists who preferred to work in marble and other forms like the jewelry piece on the left.

This is not to say that Romans did not make their own original contributions to art — particularly in the field of architecture. However, Roman structural engineering "was more secular and utilitarian" and tended towards grandeur and scale more so than had been the case in Greece. Romans invented concrete and this allowed them to perfect the arch, vault and dome. These engineering feats made it possible for the much grander architecture Romans favored.

Relief sculpture, mosaic and fresco developed into an important feature of patrician domestic decoration, examples of which survive at Pompeii and Herculaneum.

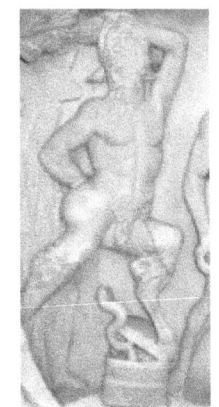

The Romans adopted the gods of the Greek pantheon and renamed them. Zeus became Jupiter, Athena became Artemis, Hermes was rechristened as Mercury and so forth. Not to be left out, Pan was imported by the Romans as Faunus (sometimes called "Lupercalis) who appears in the relief sculpture appearing on the lower right as seen in the ruins of the Colosseum in Rome and the broach on the previous page.

Once again, satyrs and fauns were not always depicted with cloven hoofed feet. In many cases appearing sans the hairy body of a wild animal — owing to the Roman adoption of the Greek philosopher Plato's attitude towards physical beauty associated with good and ugliness with evil.

The extensive use of wall painting at the time demonstrated that the Romans harbored a keen interest in landscape and illustrations of scenes from myth and legend and the Roman technique in rendering these images were more advanced in the use of elementary perspective technique than had been accomplished by the Greeks.

In this medium, there are numerous examples of satyrs, fauns and the Roman god Baccus (the Greek's god Dionysos) who took on Silenus' duties at the wine press and as the happy drunk.

However, it is a new development in architectural decoration that will be of keen interest to Bigfoot enthusiasts that apparently first appeared in the second century of the Roman era. This form is referred to as "The Green Man."

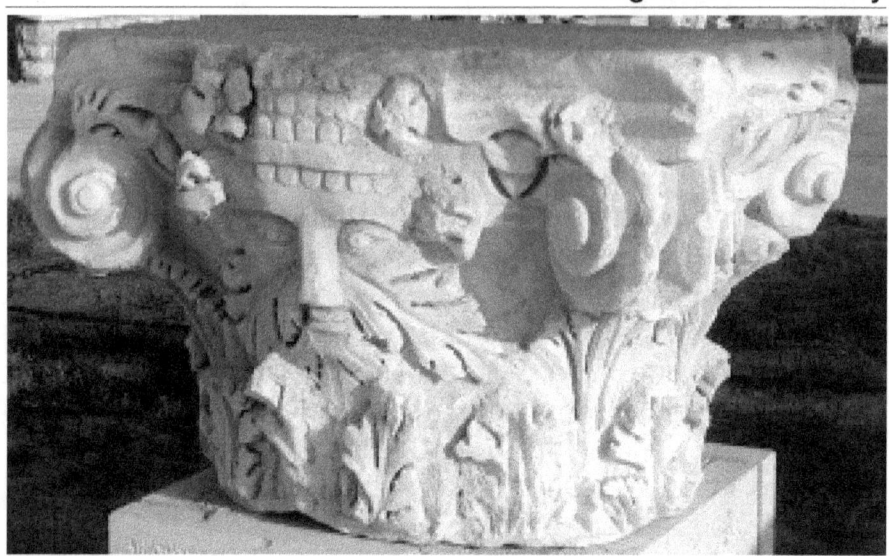

Fig. 15 - *Roman Architectural Column Capital depicting a "Green Man" face among an acanthus leaf motif. Face images such as this appeared in Roman art as early as the 2nd century AD.*

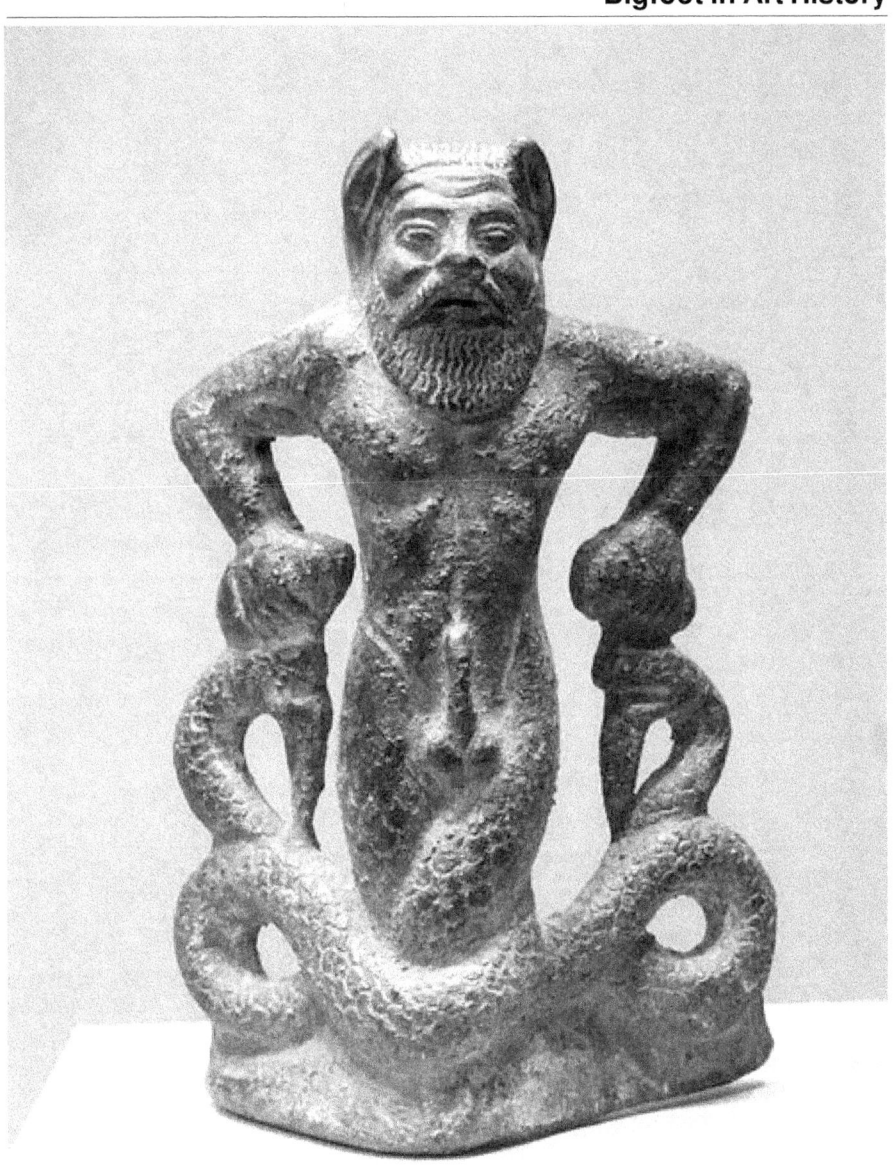

Typhon Foot Element, circa 500 BC, Etruscan, bronze - Cleveland Museum of Art. Typhopn "was the most deadly monster of Greek mythology. The last son of Gaia, fathered by Tartarus, he was known as the 'Father of All Monsters'; his wife Echidna was likewise the 'Mother of All Monsters.'" This piece, however, is of Roman design.

BIGFOOT IN BYZANTINE ART

Bigfoot in Byzantine Art

After the Roman empire was split into Western and Eastern divisions by the emperor Constantine in the 4th century AD and with the acceptance of Christianity as the state religion, art in the Eastern empire, newly based in the Greek town of Byzantium (Constantinople — today's Istanbul, Turkey) became a distinctive style that tended to feature Christian themes and state propaganda promoting the ruling class.

Roman art forms were largely preserved and advanced, but as the Christian church grappled with reconciling their creed with the Church's new political status, artists apparently avoided employing subjects in their work not in favor with the church or state. This is most likely the reason that I have not been particularly successful in locating many depictions of BHPs in the art of the Byzantine Period.

I did come across one part of a 50 section floor mosaic of the period from a church in the old city of Olbia (Qasr, Libya) which includes the image on the right, now in a museum near its original home. Vandals had sacked and occupied sections of northern Africa in the middle of the fifth and first 25 years of the sixth century AD, including Olbia. However the Byzantine emperor, Justinian, refounded the city in 539 AD.

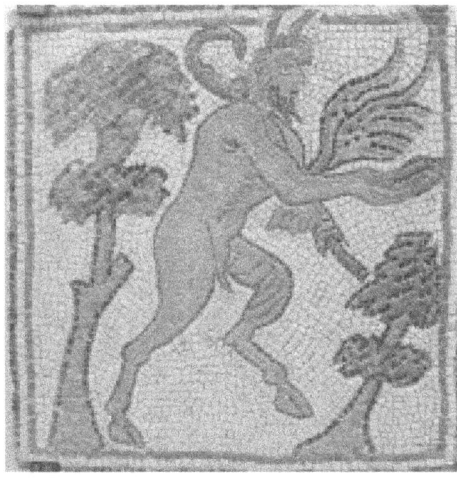

The image is another satyr creature, this time carrying off what appears to be some sort of bird. The significance of the piece I derive from the context in which it was created. The entirety of the floor mosaic from the church represents events associated with the founding of the city. So I find it interesting that this scene would appear among others which ostensibly depict realistic images and not fantasy illustrations from myth, legend or folklore.

This artifact below was recently found in England at the Roman amphitheater being excavated in Chester.

The piece is, as yet, undated, but probably dates to late in the Roman occupation of the British Isles — circa mid 5th century AD — perhaps a bit later. So I am including this illustration under Byzantine art even though Britannia was administered under the Western Roman Empire at the time.

Again, we see the wildman's face, but this time as a decorative ornament worn on clothing, demonstrating that the use of this sort of imagery was more widespread than in architecture alone by this time period.

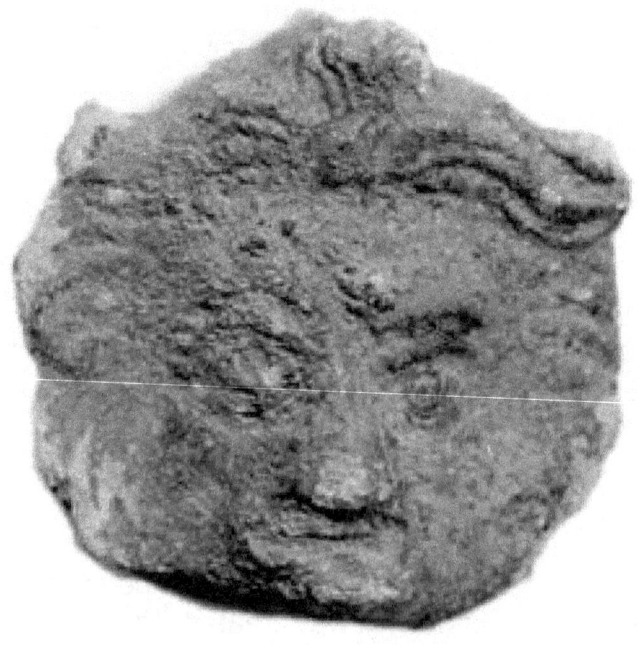

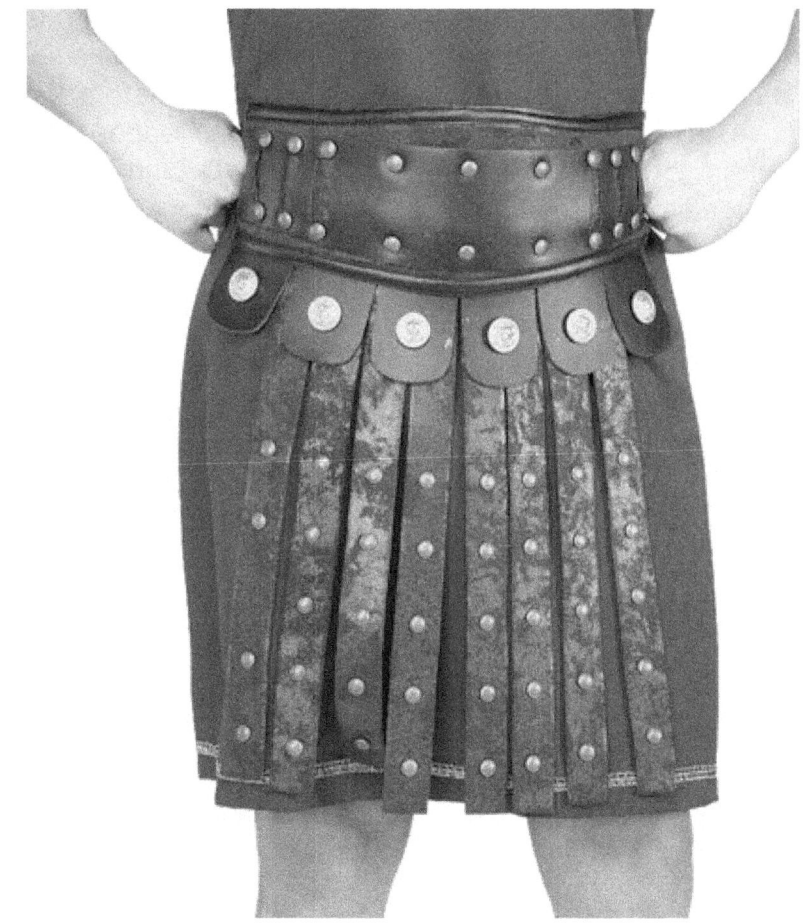

The copper-alloy stud with the green man or "wodewose" face (previous page) was probably a decoration on a Roman soldier's apron — the length of vertical leather straps (see photo above) that hung from his midsection — or as a clip for robes gathered over the shoulder, or possibly a Roman's belt buckle.

The Byzantine tapestry (appearing on the next page) is crafted out of wool and linen. It came from a 6th century AD source in Egypt and is a depiction of the Greek goddess, Hestia, the goddess of the hearth. The tapestry has dimensions measuring 44 by 53 inches.

It is titled (in Greek) "Hestia Polyolbos" which translates as Hestia full of Blessings. Her Roman equivalent, Vesta, was also the goddess of the hearth and home but had a slightly different domain in that Vesta has more publicly social duties. The reader will likely have heard of "Vestal Virgins" -- these were attendants at the temples dedicated to Vesta. Like Hestia, Vesta was sworn to a chaste life.

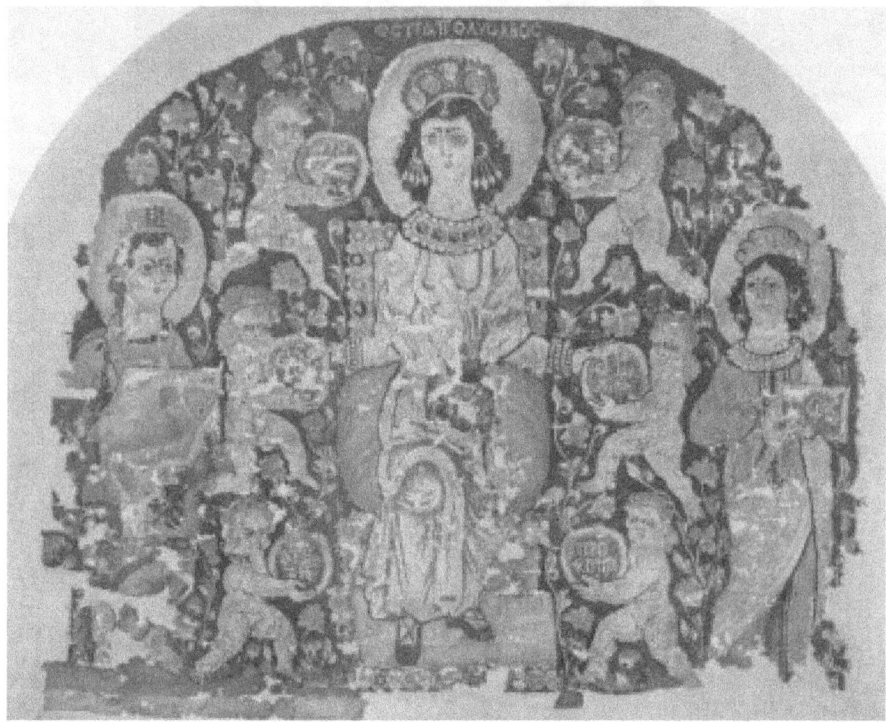

Fig. 16 - *"Hestia full of Blessings" tapistry from Egypt, 6th century AD, Dumbarton Oaks Collection, Washington D.C.*

In the tapestry, you'll see that Hestia is attended by two wildmen (Bigfoot) near her head at the center top of the artifact.

The reader will recall that the Egyptian god, Bes, was similarly charged with the protection of hearth and home. Thus, this depiction may be intended to convey that duty or, perhaps, that the more contemporary manifestation of Bes is simply bridging the distance in time between the earlier demigod and the duties and responsibilities of the newer goddess.

The Byzantine Empire (or Eastern Roman Empire) despite the demise of its Western Roman counterpart, continued to prosper and thrive for about a thousand years until it eventually fell to the Ottoman Turks in 1453.

The Byzantine culture was exported to its neighboring lands and empires. Byzantine art in the form of paintings, illuminated books, and textiles were frequently taken to the West and into Asia as diplomatic gifts. Byzantine artistic style and traditions were also transmitted by artists who studied in Constantinople and by scholars, and soldiers and we will see this influence manifest itself in later artistic periods.

BIGFOOT IN ISLAMIC ART

Bigfoot in Islamic Art

Islamic art falls into three types: renditions of the Qan in kufic or cursive writing, artistic expressions of nature (animals and foliage) or geometric designs independent of the human figure (not to say that human depictions were absent from Islamic art), and an equality of these genres.

While I have seen examples of fantasy creatures in Islamic art, depictions like the wildman below are otherwise quite rare, if not nonexistent, in Islamic Art. This one is from the Alhambra Palace in Granada, Spain, a Moorish architectural masterpiece of its era. Located in the Hall of Kings at the east rear of the Court of Lions is the Sala de los Justica — subdivided into seven alcoves with domed ceilings. Among them you'll find the image of a knight saving a "fair maiden" from what appears to be a wildman or Bigfoot painted on leather. Alhambra was begun in 1238 AD and served as the last bastion of the Spanish Moslems on the Iberian peninsula. The facility was both a fortress and palace and served as a center of

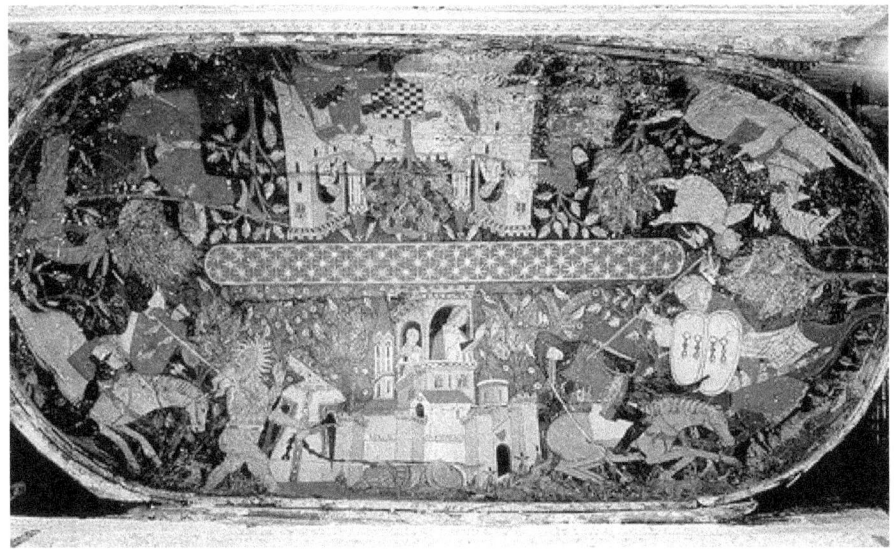

Fig. 17 - *Ceiling painting on leather, Sala de los Justica, Hall of Kings, Alhambra, Spain*

government until early in 1492 when Granada surrendered to Ferdinand II of Aragon and Isabella I of Castile.

Interesting aspects of this painting are many — as if the startling image of a hairy wildman isn't sufficient. The background has clear Islamic art motifs, while the hero riding to the rescue is depicted as a Templar Knight (his shield hides what is undoubtedly a red cross on his white tunic) of the First Crusade — a foe of the Islamic

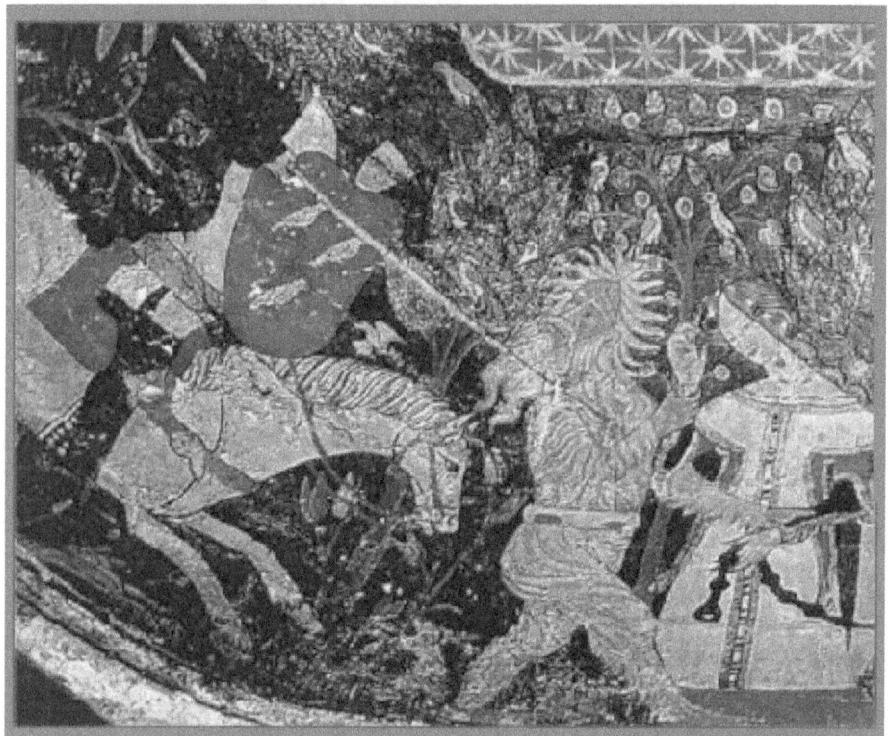

forces that occupied the Holy Land at that time. The painting is dated to between 1377 and 1391 AD — about 300 years after the start of the First Crusade.

Given the composition of the art, it is pretty obvious that wildmen, at least in medieval Spain, were again considered a threat to the virtue of womanhood by the males of the population of the day.

Therefore, I return to my previous position that these animals, assuming they're reality, were compelled to shun human contact by the hostile actions of men. Perhaps deservedly so if they were attempting to abduct women and children for nefarious reasons. Nevertheless, I also find it extremely interesting that this subject would rise to this level of importance that it was chosen to grace such an important Islamic structure as Alhambra.

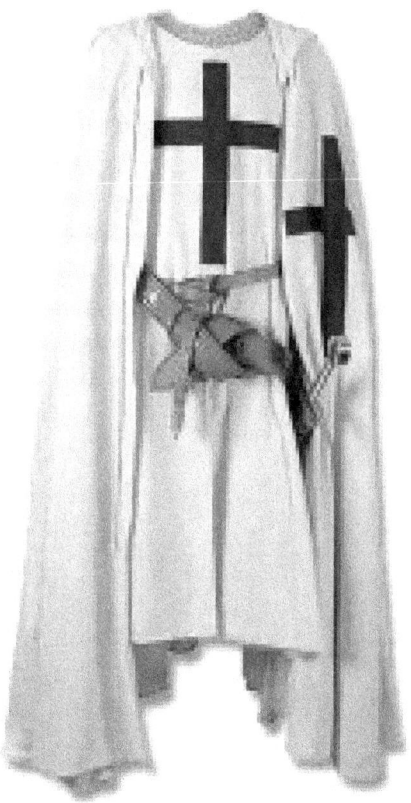

Fig. 18 - *At the council of Troy in 1128, the Templar Order was confirmed by Pope Honorius II. The Knights received the white vestment as a symbol of purity of their life, to which Pope Eugenius added the red cross in 1146. (This is a replica of their uniform). In volume 2 of this work, we will review the Green Man phenomena found at the Rosslyn Chapel in Scotland.*

BIGFOOT IN EARLY MEDIEVAL ART

Bigfoot in Early Medieval Art

In Early Medieval Europe, between the first millennium and 1200 AD, the Byzantine Empire was preoccupied with Muslim invaders (who also threatened the Western and Central European homeland).

Pope Gregory VII called for the Christian Military to assist in the defense of the Byzantine Empire in the east in 1074. Just 20 years later, Pope Urban I (in 1095) called for the first crusade to liberate the holy city of Jerusalem and the Holy Land from Muslim control and to free the Christians living in the Eastern Empire from Islamic rule.

Although Europe was in political turmoil, artists of the Early Medieval period did manage to craft some impressive artistic work such as the column capital shown below.

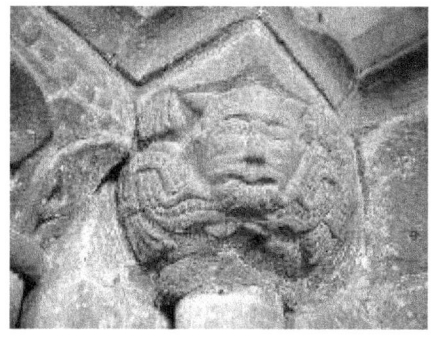

You'll note that our friend, the Green Man (or as would be more correct in this time frame, the "wodewose") again appeared as a decorative feature in architecture. This carving shows the mystery face with acanthus growing out of its mouth instead of as a foliage cover.

This depiction became common after the Early Medieval period and probably gave rise to the contemporary colloquial term "Tree Eater" for a Bigfoot in parts of Southeastern Europe. Indeed, the term 'wodewose' actually originates from the Anglo-Saxon word "wudewasa" now meaning a Bigfoot like animal in Northern Europe. This compound word is derived from the word "wudu" a late Old English term generally meaning "wood" (or sometimes "mad") and "wasa" which translates as "man". Thus "wudewasa" quite literally means a 'man-of-the-woods', or "wild man" further supporting my conjecture that these images do relate to an actual wildman and not a fictional creature -- although mainstream scholars will undoubtedly take exception to this contention.

The Green Man, according to Norman John Grenville Pounds, "In literature (of the Medieval Period and thereafter) he is seen as living in remote places, especially in forests, where his great strength, epitomized in his covering of hair, served him well in his struggle with wild beasts. He bore no relationship to anything in Christianity, and probably derived from pagan nature myths. Yet no attempt was ever made to eradicate him from the iconography of the Christian Church."[6]

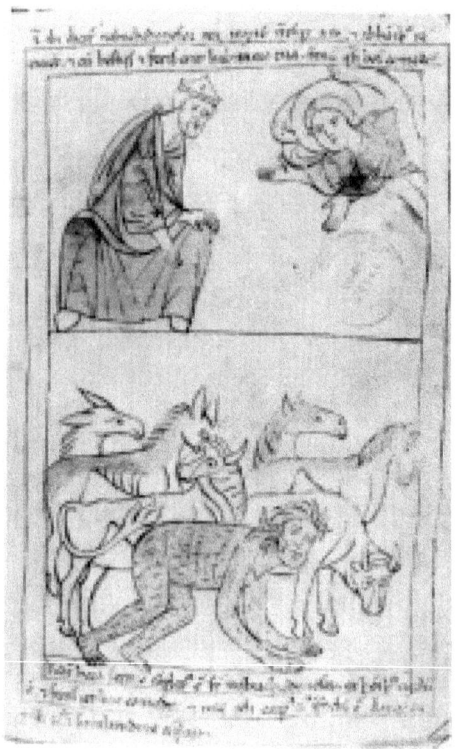

Grenville's point is important in examining Bigfoot-like animals appearing in art history from this era forward as other BHP creatures, notably fauns and satyrs, did not fare as well with artists due to the growing influence of the church during the artistic eras which followed.

This is reflected in the column capital appearing in Figurer 20 on the next page from the Church of St Aignan in Orleans, Loiret, France. It shows a wildman amongst the beasts in this Gothic Period Architecture.

Fig. 19 - *A manuscript illumination from the Bible of King Sancho el Fuente, Navarre, Spain circa 1194. The depiction is that of King Nebuchadrezzar cast out amongst the beasts. Note that the King appears to be striken with unusual hairyness and on all fours. This is a common theme from Medieval and Renaissance work in which BHPs appear.*

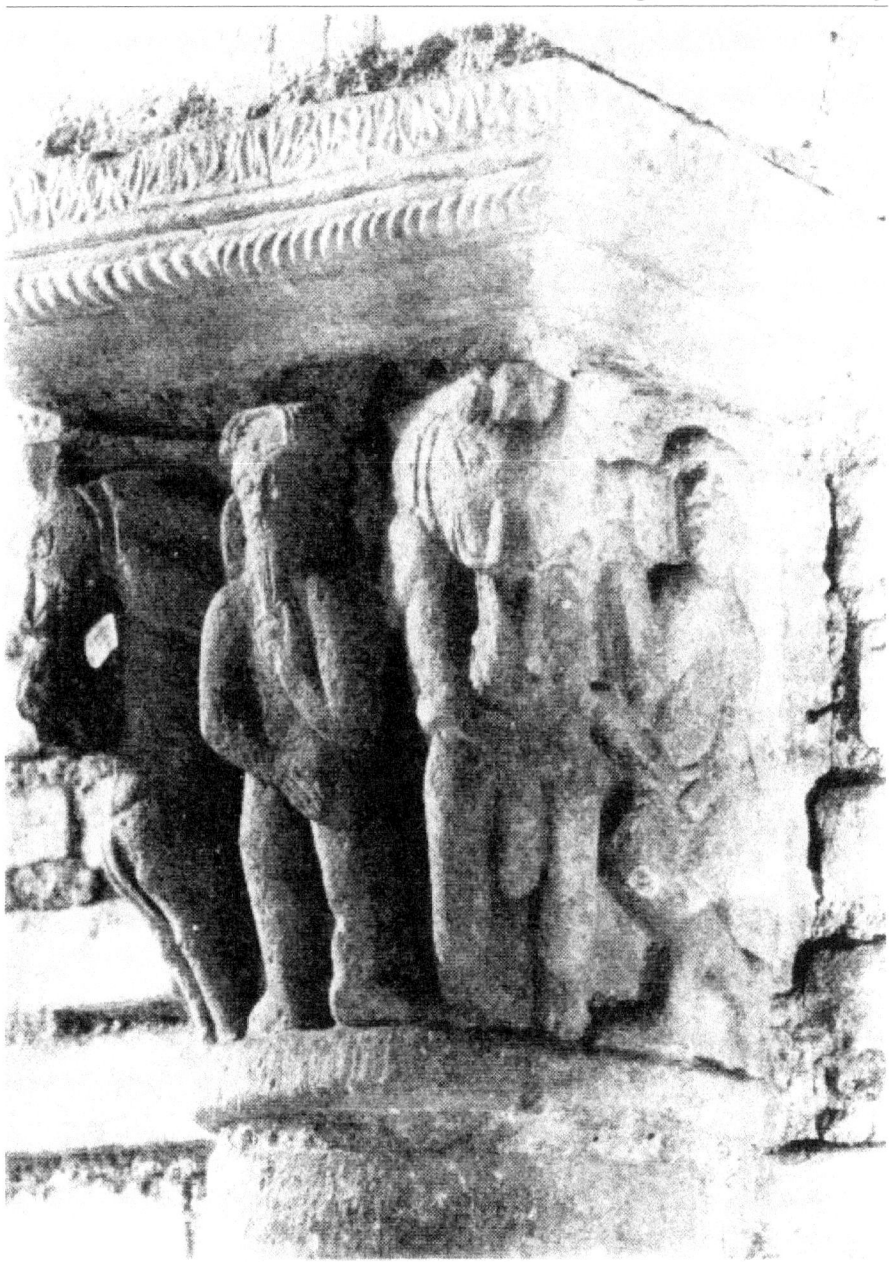

Fig. 20 - *Wildman amongst the beasts, column capital from Saint-Aigman, circa 1000 AD*

BIGFOOT IN ROMANESQUE ART

Bigfoot in Romanesque Art

The Romanesque style is the era that describes the art and architecture developed in Europe during the late 10th century. In England, the Romanesque style of art is traditionally referred to as the "Norman Period." The Romanesque style evolved into the Gothic forms by the mid-12th century AD.

We have reviewed images of the so-called "Green Man" appearing on the carved marble double capital found in a church located in the Toulouse region of France that dated to around 1100 AD and the "Wildman Among Beasts" capital from St Aignan in Orleans, Loiret, France that is somewhat more contemporary.

As the Medieval artistic styles developed, the Green Man and Wildman images underwent a number of notable transformations. Over a period of about 150 years beginning with the Romanesque period the Green Man evolved from a decorative border element or flourish on a page in written works to a more fundamental art form associated with the revival of three-dimensional sculptural work. So this subject appeared much has it had originally been depicted in the classical Roman architecture we have reviewed previously.. However the Green Man emerged over time as more than a mere face concealed amid flora.

As we have discovered, there are many aspects to foliate head carvings (Green

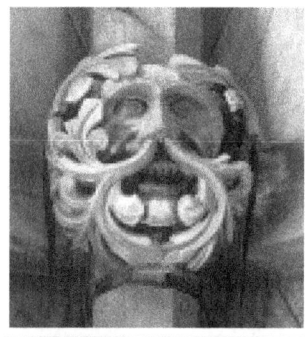
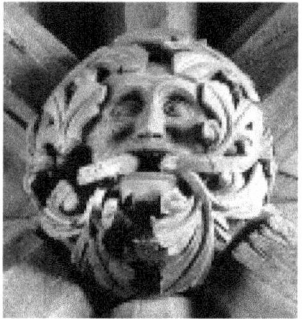

Fig. 21 - *Dated between 1180 and 1280 AD, these roof bosses found at Warmington Church (Northamptonshire, England) depict human faces with strongly defined features, surrounded by naturalistic foliage. They are typical examples the 'Green Man'.*

Men) and many examples of them can be found in art and architecture from around the world.

During the Romanesque era in Europe, Green Men were usually carved out of wood or stone in addition to their continued appearances in manuscript illustrations, illuminations and so forth — as had primarily been the case during the Early Medieval time frame that preceded the Romanesque period.

Green Men carvings are not considered "high art" in the sense that they were not crafted by an artist elite of the day. They were almost exclusively the product of stone masons and wood carvers – the Medieval working class. So these images took their inspiration from the experience of these "common folk" and thus reflect possible encounters with their bipedal, hairy counterparts of the forest.

From our perspective, the Green Men offer us a significant insight into the perceptions of the non-literate people of the time who are conspicuously omitted from most official reports of medieval life. As a rule these records were penned by, or for, the aristocracy or the clergy and devoid of the common man's mundane perspectives.

Aside from foliate head carvings (or Green Men), the more anatomically complete sculptural artworks of the Romanesque period often took the form of gargoyles, cernunnos and hybrids.

Gargoyles are waterspouts projecting from a roof gutter or upper part of a structure to direct water away from its walls or foundations. This was done to protect the mortar and the stonework of buildings from erosion. Gargoyles forms are widespread on structures built during the Romanesque and Gothic periods, but had its origins with Classical Greek architecture.

Human gargoyles were often bizarre and sometimes preposterous – if not pathetic images. Their unusual, and often grotesque, physical characteristics are probably connected with the medieval concept that attributed physical ugliness and sickness to demonic possession and evil.

Another pagan motif to be found in churches arose from Celtic mythology. In pre-Christian times the Cernunnos, the old horned god of the woodlands resembling the classical Greek satyr and Roman Pan, was the lord of all animals. Over time, the influence of the church transformed Cernunnos into an artistic manifestation of the devil.[7]

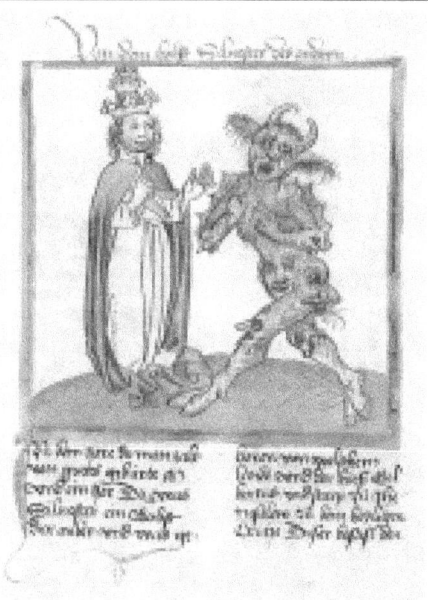

Fig. 2 - *Pope Sylvester II and a cernunnos portrayed as the devil. Circa 1000 AD.*

Rabanus Maurus, an 8th century theologian, held that the Green Man represented "the sins of the flesh, lustful wicked men doomed to eternal damnation."

Expanding on Maurus' original idea the bishop, Isidorus of Sevilla, who lived between 570 and 636 AD wrote in his book *Ethymologiae* that "criminals, as a result of their offences made themselves slaves to demonic powers." These offenders were required by the devil to eat magical plants which transformed them into a variety of different animals or hybrids.[8]

This belief most likely formed the basis for the medieval explanation of anthropomorphic hybrids and probably gave rise to the concept of "familiars" known in witchcraft and sorcerer folklore.

A hybrid is the combination of two or more different animals. Hybrids are closely akin to the anthropomorphized images of Egyptian deities that we already examined in Part 1 of Bigfoot in Art History. However, during the Romanesque and Gothic periods in Europe, hybrids were characterized as hirsute or as having the extremities of animals.

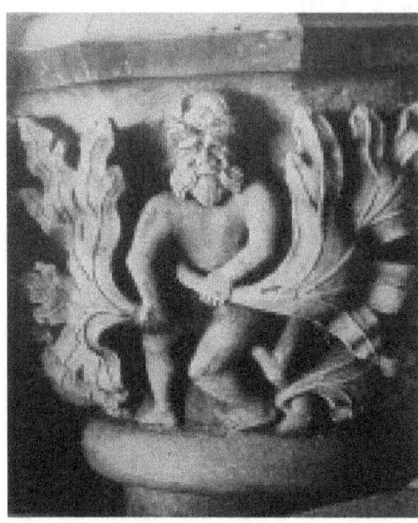

Fig. 23 - *A more anatomically complete example of the Green Man found in York, England (c. 1069 AD)*

The idea of feral people living in the woodlands was not an unusual concept during this time and this thinking was likely based on actual fact as the circumstance appears widely in art, literature and folklore throughout the "Age of Enlightenment."

It was not at all unusual for people who were different from their fellows in physical appearance, those ostracized for one reason or another, or infected with some sort of communicable disease (or thought to be contagious) to be banished from the normal precincts of "civilized" society. This practice was used for millennia before the eras covered in this discussion.

As animals were regarded to be lower forms of life wild people closely resembling them were regarded as degenerated humans who had allowed the "beast within" to manifest itself through them.

Indeed, this explanation for the "meaning" of BHP images in artwork persists to this day. However, the application of the explanation, as you see, is really a matter of contention as the "chicken and the egg" equivocation clearly applies here, and it is very likely that "outsiders" existed before the lore about them arose much as children frequently make up stories about "strange" or recluse neighbors today.

Wild people were also viewed as sinners (in the Isidorus of Sevilla meaning of the word) upon whom God had heaped his punishment. Thus, depictions of them were sanctioned by the church in that they served as a warning to potential transgressors.

Wildmen of the woods were typically depicted as naked hirsute people who carried a club. They were required to kill animals and skin them in order to fashion clothes – if they wore clothing at all.

Legends regarding wild people vary but, in at least one version, these feral people were said to live high in the trees in India in order to avoid being attacked by wild animals. This lore may have originated with ape species – possibly orangutans — living in the subcontinent of Asia and result from an exaggeration of factual accounts.

One notable legend of the period occurred in the English city of Orford sometime between 1167 and 1204 AD. At the time the port of Orford, located on the East coast of England, was an affluent city. King Henry II had built his castle there as a fortress against the underhanded Hugh Bigod of Bungay.

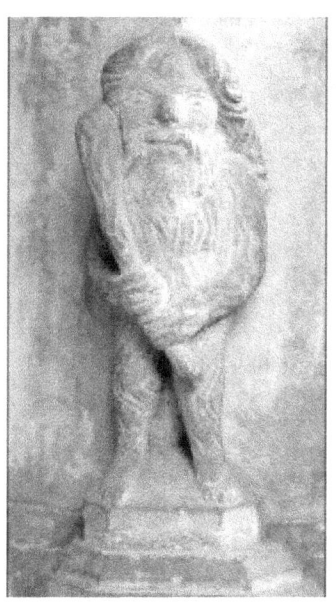

The event I'm about to related was recorded by Ralph of Coggeshall, the Abbott's chronicler, in his *History of Orford* written in 1207.

While fishing off the coast of Orford, a group of fishermen caught an unusual visitor in their nets. When they pulled the nets back on board their boats they found a large creature tangled in among the fish. The visitor was a "man" staring angrily back at them.

Fig 24 - The Orford Merman. Located at St. Bartholomew's Church in Orford, England. c. 1165.

The "merman" is described by Coggeshall as being "naked, but with a hairy body, as having a long straggly beard and the top of his head being completely bald."

The wildman was mute and initially violent so the fishermen restrained him and took him back to the port and Orford castle where the custodian, Bartholomew de Gladville, kept him as a prisoner.

In mythology, mermaids are generally described as being great beauties with a charm that they use to lure sailors to their deaths. Mermen, on the other hand, are usually said to be ugly and less refined. The few merman stories that exist suggest Mermen have little interest in mankind. Most attribute them with powers to create fearsome storms and to sink ships as revenge for men's mistreatment of their adored mermaids.

However, not all lore portrays Mermen in this manner; Benwell describes a Scandinavian merman known as "Havmand" as a handsome person with a green or black beard who lived on the cliffs and shore hillside as well as in the sea. Benwell goes on to say that Havmand was regarded as a beneficent creature.[9] Mermen have also been credited with warning men of impending peril.

On the downside, Mermen have also been accused of kidnapping young sailors and taking them below the sea where the captives would drown. Then again, some of these captives were reported to have lived "happily ever after" upon gaining a miraculous ability to survive under water.

Getting back to the Orford merman, the captive eagerly ate whatever food was given to him. De Gladville and others tried time after time to question the merman but the creature could, or would, only voice grunts and odd gurgles — even when his captors tortured him by suspending him by his feet.

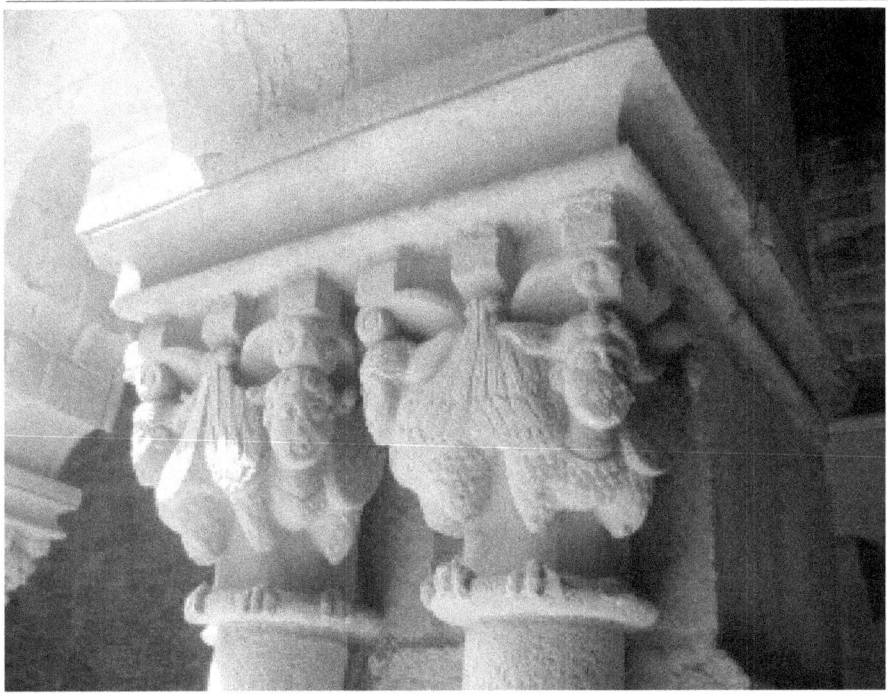

Fig. 25 - *Column capitals from the church of San Pablo del Campo, cloister area, located in Barcelona, Spain. Note the exquisite decorative detail of the wildmen carvings of the column sculptures. c. 1117 AD.*

He had a peculiar habit when consuming raw fish — he pressed it between his hands until all the juices were squeezed out and drank the fluid.

When he was taken into a church, the merman showed no sign of worship or religious belief – this the townspeople likely found barbaric if not totally pagan. The merman went to bed at sunset and remained there until the sun came up each day.

The townspeople allowed the merman to swim in the sea, but surrounded him with three lines of guarded nets. He would dive beneath the nets and come up over and over again – apparently looking for an escape route. However, temporarily resigned to his captivity, he eventually came back of his own accord.

The story goes on to say that the merman did eventually escape and was never seen by the Orford people again.

One of the more interesting aspects of this story is that it is told by Coggeshall in a very factual manner. There isn't any hint of the imaginary events, storms or the mysterious deaths at sea, generally ascribed to conventional merman lore.

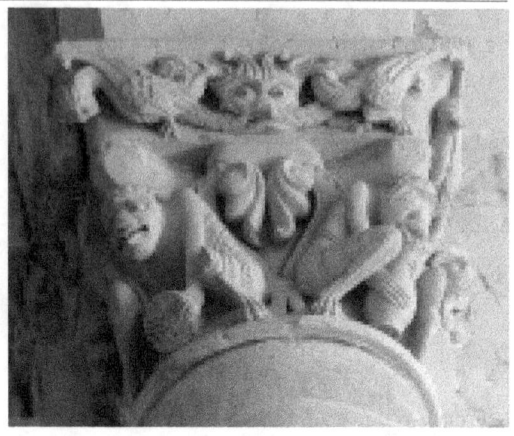

Fig. 26 - A Gothic column capital from the 11th century Romanesque church of Notre Dame de Cunault, at Maine-et-Loire, France depicts a wildman (left), cernunnos (as the Green Man - center top) and a hybrid (right).

The tale of the Orford merman is reminiscent of the famed story of Zana – the female Almasty captured in the Republic of Georgia during the late 19th century. Many of the traits ascribed to the merman were also exhibited by Zana – according to the documented accounts of her capture and captivity.

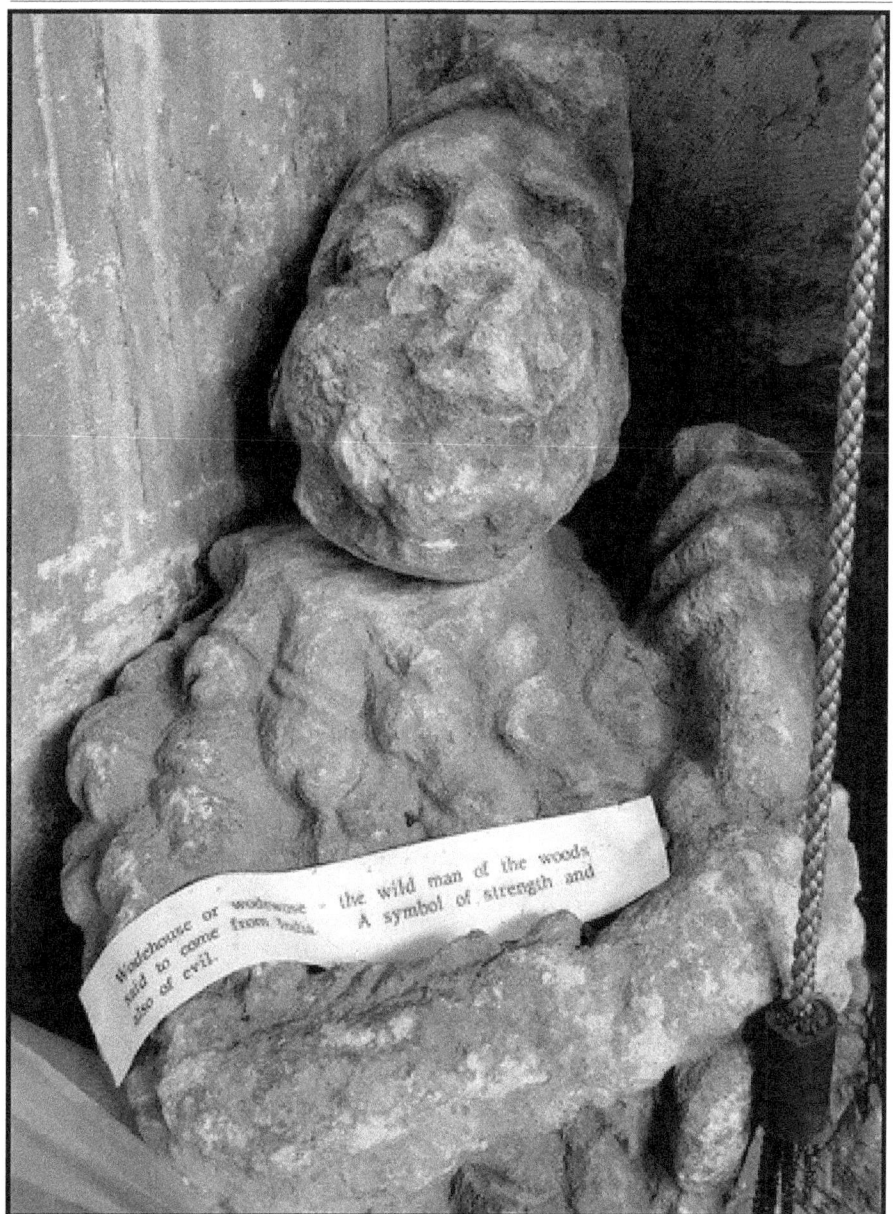

Fig. 27 - *Wildman of the Woods found at St Mary Church, Woolpit, Suffolk, England. c. 1200 AD.*

BIGFOOT IN
GOTHIC ART

Bigfoot in Gothic Art

Gothic art is the term applied to the artistic style of architecture, painting, and sculpture which thrived in Western Europe during the later part of the Medieval Period from the 12th to the 15th centuries. For about 350 years it evolved from a religious art form towards a more worldly and natural style.

The term "Gothic" was first applied to the movement during the Renaissance when critics condemned the art form as vulgar and named it after the Goth tribes that ransacked the Roman Empire during the 5th century AD.

The principal Gothic art media were architecture, sculpture, painted panels, stained glass, fresco and illuminations in manuscripts.

The Gothic architectural style began in France fostered by the Romanesque Period architecture of the mid-12th century and blended other structural technologies.

Fig. 28 - *Stonework detail of the Southwell Minster Chapter House showing a Green Man. Southwell,*

The Romans had developed their vaulting system proficiency during the 1st century AD. This technology included both the barrel and the groin vault — the groin vault being an intersection of two barrel vaults. This produces a structure that features arched openings on all four sides, and therefore divides the enclosed space into sections known as "bays."

This methodology was revived by Romanesque architects and formed the basis for the more complex and diverse kind of vault construction developed during the Gothic Period.

In fact, the main achievement of Gothic architecture was the taking of the archaic and heavier vault forms of Romanesque architecture (which employed a solid stone vault) and developing a lighter, distinguished Gothic design that incorporated elements from the Islamic pointed arch and the cross-ribbed vault.[10]

Many older Romanesque cathedrals were destroyed by fire over time. So this new, improved architectural technology became a viable solution to the church's general need to rebuild these assets.

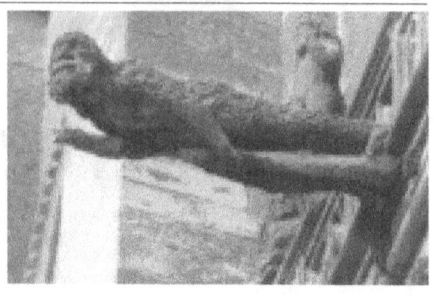

Fig. 29 - On of the many gargoyles you'll find adorning the Cathedral of Notre Dame in Paris, France. This one is of a wildman while most are of fantastic creatures like chimeras. dragons or hybrids. c. 1163 AD.

The advent of Gothic architecture began with the construction of the Abbey Church of Saint-Denis begun about 1130 AD. The style was then employed in the construction of other cathedrals during the 12th century including (in chronological order) Sens (c. 1140), Noyons (c. 1150), Senlis (c. 1151), Paris (c. 1163), Laon (c. 1165), Chartres (c. 1194), Reims (c 1211) and Amiens (c. 1220).

By the 13th century, Gothic architecture had become fully embraced in much of Western Europe — owing to the stone masons and other artisans who were free to travel to ply their trade.

Thus, as a consequence of the more cosmopolitan economy of the period, the creation of the Gothic style cathedrals (as well as other religious and secular structures) in major cities and towns in Britain, Spain, and Germany became commonplace.

Gothic sculpture is closely linked with the introduction of Gothic architecture. As a continuation of sculptural forms defined by the Romanesque period, Gothic sculpture included the decoration of architectural features like columns, reliefs, friezes, door jambs, gates

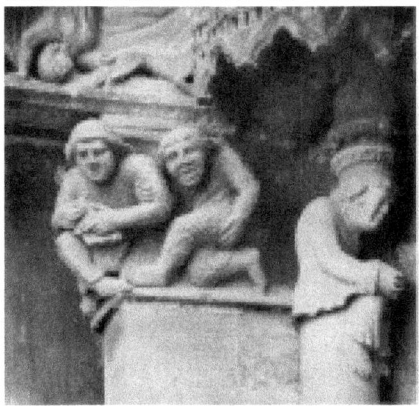

Fig. 30 - *A column capital from the cathedral Notre-Dame, located in Semur-en-Auxois, Côte-d'or, France features this 13th century image of a wildman and his human companion.*

and tombs — as was the case with its antecedent style. However, Gothic sculpture introduced new genres into the medium as well including religious statuary, altarpieces and heraldic stones.

The more colossal and decorative sculptural work was generally carved out of stone, marble, or alabaster and was occasionally detailed with paint.

Gothic period sculpture also included fine woodcarving containing sophisticated elements in choir stalls, tracery, finials, panels and the slender, pointed apex set on top of buttresses and roof gables called "pinnacles" in the more massive buildings.

The Gothic style of painting began in Italy and rapidly spread throughout most of Europe and remained the dominant style for about 200 years. In contrast to the older Romanesque and Byzantine art forms the movement was distinguished by the use of dark toned oils and an increasing degree of naturalism.[11]

By the late 14th century Gothic painting had started to reflect Renaissance ideals and integrated the Italian and Northern European styles resulting in a method that amalgamated a variety of different ideas, thoughts, and techniques. The combined form became known as the "International Gothic style." It was during this phase of development that the Gothic Style of painting gained great popularity in France, Italy, England, Germany, Austria, and Bohemia.

Toward the end of the 15th century, as the Gothic Style began fade, some artists in parts of Northern Europe resisted the progressive Renaissance influences and stubbornly held on to the Gothic tradition.

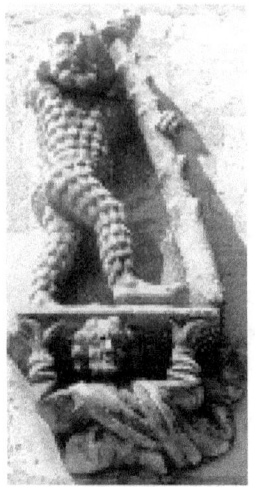

Fig.31 - In Ay Beaulieu-sur-Dordogne, France you'll find a building with gothic carvings of Green Men and this Wild Man with long club.

Fig.32 - The City of Linz, Austria is not lacking in gothic era wildman like this relief.

Because of this, defining the end of the Gothic Period becomes difficult and its time line thus overlaps both the Italian and the Northern Renaissance period.[12]

Now that we've established a background context relative to artistic developments during the Gothic Period, we should discuss a framework for understanding the perspective of the medieval mind as it perceived creatures like the wildman.

The wodewose (AKA the wildman, woose, woot, tree-eater, and quite a few other colloquial designations) in the iconography of the medieval time frame represented an intensely significant feature in the visual arts repertoire of the day and that society's view of primitive life.[13]

In this pre-Darwin culture, even the privileged literate did not have a scientific context within which to comprehend evolution – much less the common, illiterate populace. Thus, the people of the era relied largely on religious belief and the local clergy's interpretation of the Bible for their understanding of the natural world. The church's perspective was sometimes confused with, and in many cases confounded by, popular oral mythology and folklore that generally had its roots in paganism – which some scholars have chosen to regard as mere superstition.

"Essentially, the wildman had an unclear status in medieval thought – there was confusion over his position in God's creation. Since medieval thought emphasized the purity of all species, the wildman could not be conceived of as a half-evolved human or as a stage in the progression of humans to civilization."[14]

The wildman "was (the) closest that medieval scholars came to understanding humanity's primeval beginnings. Thought to have come from the mountains of central Europe, the wildman was a naked hairy figure with both human and animal traits, who lived in the forest, without knowledge of metals or agriculture, eating berries, acorns, and the raw flesh of animals."[15]

Of course, this conception of the wildman also well fits the general description of what we today identify as a Bigfoot, an animal that was impossible for the people of the era to understand as anything other than a monster, magical beast or human with some sort of madness or physical affliction.

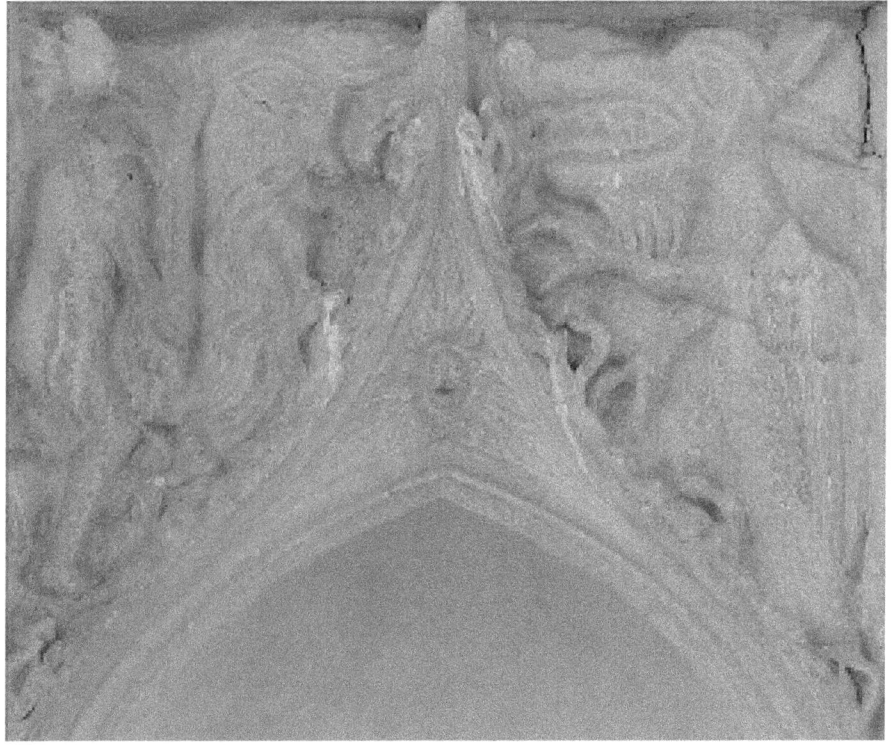

Fig. 33 - Located at St Agnes Church, Cawston, Norfolk, England, this 14th century spandrel, featuring a wild man and dragon, is one of the larger examples of this relatively common artistic theme.

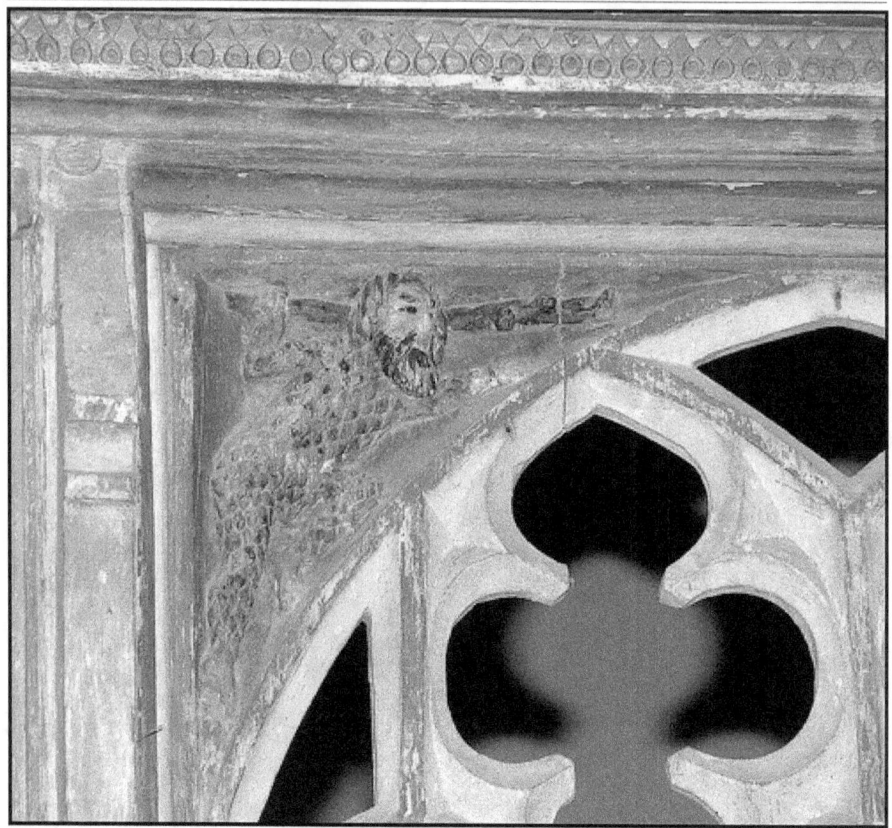

Fig. 34 - *Similar to the spandrel from St. Agnes Church, the sections of the 15th century rood screen (on this page and the next) at St Remigius, Dunston, England also features a dragon which observes a wild man creeping up on it from the opposing side. The Church was built around 1140 and the rood screen was added at a later date.*

Now that we have established a common perspective from which to assess the artistic work of the period, we can proceed to examine some of the key works of art depicting our hairy friend that I have assembled for you here.

The area between Norfolk and Suffolk, England has quite a few examples of BHP art. In the context of the day, our hairy friend is often depicted fighting a dragon. Lions were also a relatively common foe for the wildman to battle. Some scholars assert that this theme in wildman art developed

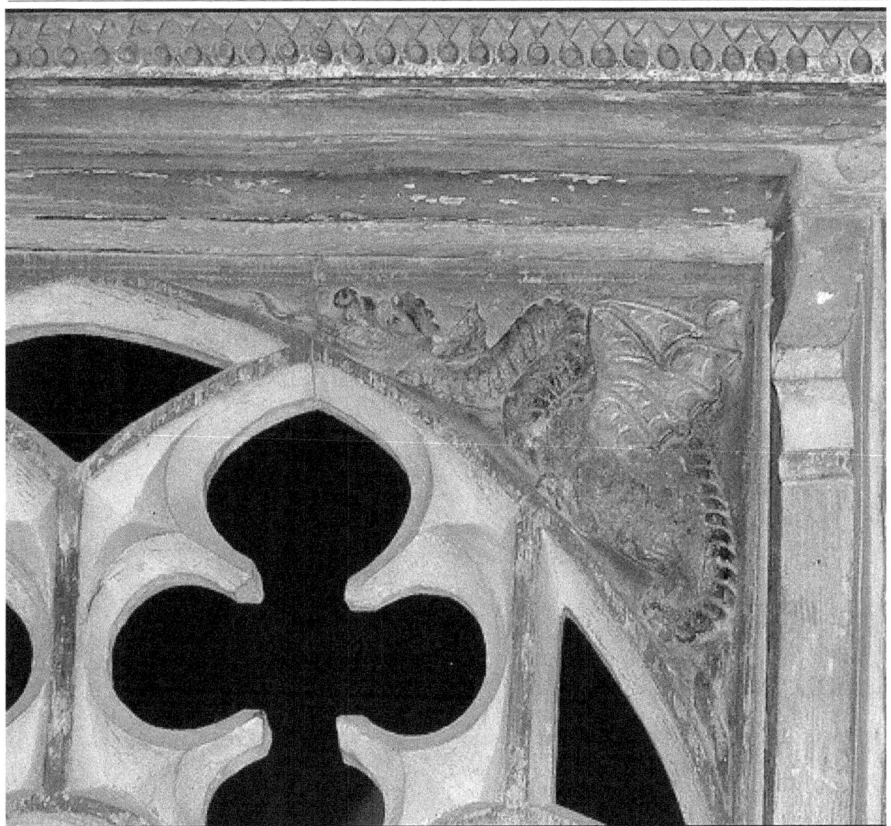

from old German folktales.

It is likely that the theme arose from the Beowulf epic poem first written in Old English prior to the 10th century AD. As you probably know, the story describes the adventures of the legendary Anglo-Saxon hero, Beowulf, which took place around of the 6th century AD.

The original manuscript of this literary work can be found in the British Library in London, England.

In the Beowulf saga, the hero (Beowulf) does battle with evil creatures, personified by Grendel the wildman, his wild woman mother (bent on revenge for the death of her hirsute son), and a dragon.

There may also be some influence from the Epic of Gilgamesh and our old friend Enkidu, the Bigfoot-like companion of the King of Ur. In this

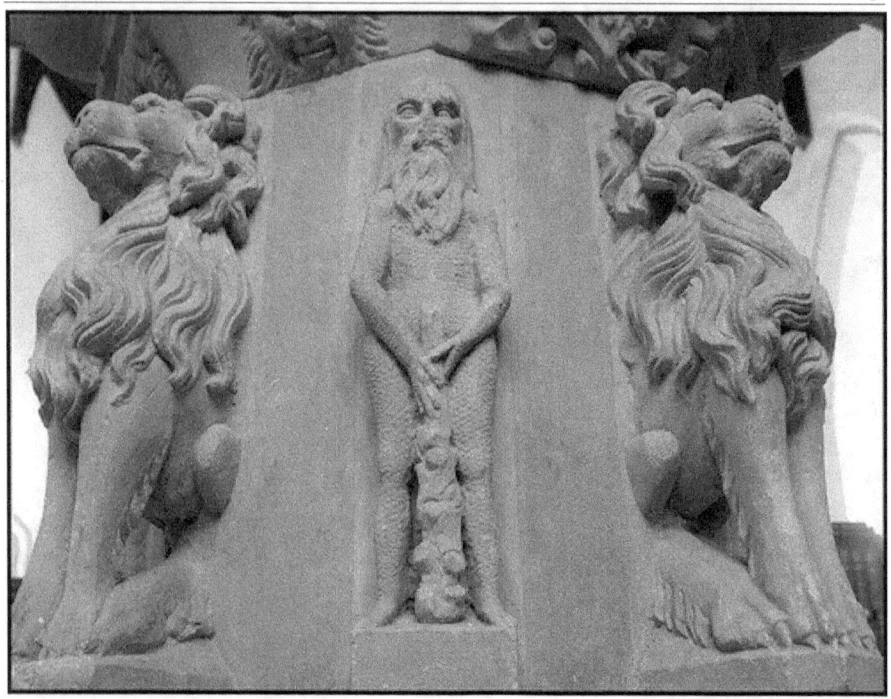

Fig. 35 - *The 15th century baptismal font is typically East Anglian. The church of St Mary in Newbourne, Suffolk, England where this example of wildman sculpture is found, dates to the 14th century,*

Sumerian heroic poem our heroes take on the dragon-like, Kur, the demon in charge of the Netherworld.

Then there is the old legend of the Basajaun in Basque mythology. The Basajaun, or in the plural Basajaunak, were said to be an ancient race of hairy wildmen who were allegedly the megalith builders of prehistoric Europe. Actually, "Basajaun" translates as meaning the "Lord of the Woods." These hefty, giant people came from the mountainous area of the Pyrenees in northeastern Spain and southwestern France.

Possessing magical powers something akin to Arabian conception of the Jinn or Genies, they also were agile and strong in addition to their hirsute animalistic appearance. The Basajaun were caretakers of the forests and the wild creatures found there, in addition to the flocks of the

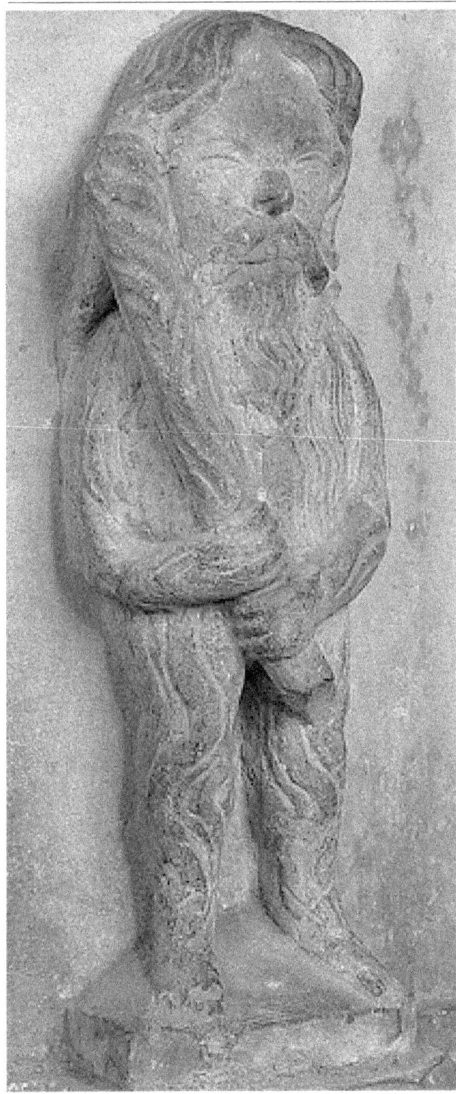

Fig. 36 - *A font at the church of the Assumption of St Mary in Haughley, England is carved with four lions and four naked hairy wildmen. Three of the wildmen carry clubs. Unlike the others, this pedestal base and bowl are carved out of limestone.*

field. They were also said to be the first farmers who taught humanity how to cultivate crops.

Some scholars speculate that the Basajuanak legends began when early Basque people encountered Neanderthal men – given that these legends are extremely old. However, that seems unlikely as the Neanderthal were a more diminutive people than the near giant Basajuanak were reported to be.

Owing to the English east coast affinity for much of the wildman subject matter, the story of the Merman of Orford probably encouraged the artistic fascination with the wodewose iconography in this area of the British Isles.

Another example of the wildman and dragon theme can be seen in the rood screen spandrel shown in figure 34. This one is also from the eastern coastal area of England and is located in the church of St. Agnes in Dunston, England.

"In religious iconography, the wildman also faces the dragon as a symbol of natural strength and fortitude available to defeat evil. . . . But we must also recall that

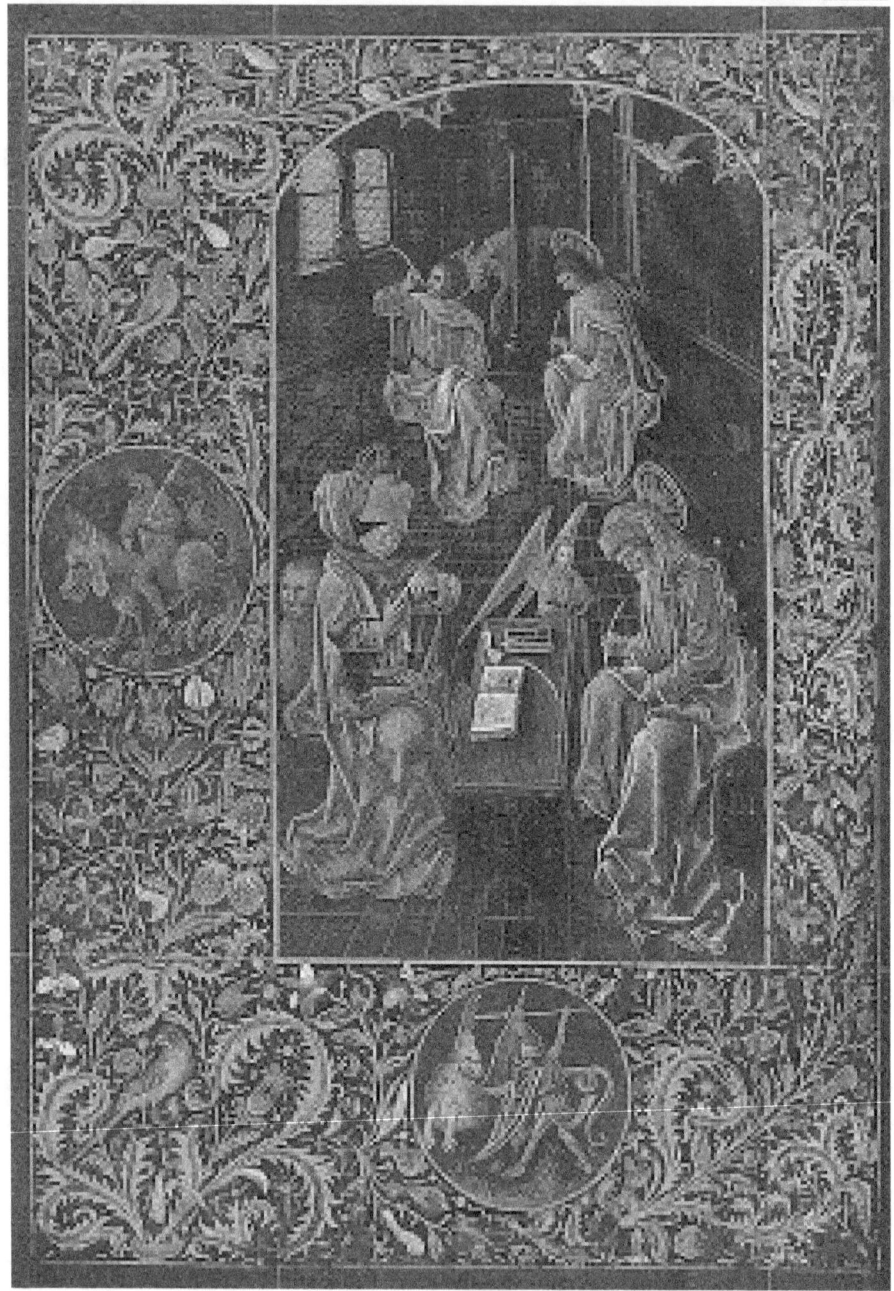

Fig. 37 - *An Illustration from the Black Book of Hours, Bruges, Flanders c.1466.*

the wildman, however strong and fertile, still remained for theology a symbol of fallen humanity."[16]

Perhaps hinting at the religious notion that baptism into "the fold" constituted a triumph over man's animal nature, the wildman was a popular subject to be carved into baptismal fonts at many churches in the Norfolk and Suffolk region of England during the Gothic Period.

The practice seems to have begun with the sculpture of the Orford merman we saw in the Romanesque chapter previously. You'll note the similarity of the Wildman's form in the examples here and with the aforementioned sculpture.

Indeed, it's interesting that the wildman image is coupled frequently, in this genre, with the evangelist saints. With the apparent exception of the example from St. Mary's of Newbourne, the wildman is not depicted in conflict with dragons or lions when not part of baptismal font decoration. Yet, and contrary to that specimen, the wildman is typically seen ready to strike a blow with his club and not at ease in his pose.

The Black Book of Hours (see preceding page), so named because the parchment upon which it was written was dyed a deep black color prior to being penned and decorated, represents a unique specimen of Gothic era art in its genre. The writing is of a gold and silver pigment, while the illustrations are painted in a style that is similar to camaieu, using but a few colors on the clothing of the subjects depicted in the drawings.

The Black Book is attributed to the artist Philippe de Mazerolles a court painter to Charles the Bold, Duke of Burgundy (1433-1477) and retained by him from 1466 AD.

You'll note the wildman, brandishing a club, astride a chimera in the circular inset appearing center left of the page.

Unfortunately the chemical composition of the black dye was not suited to the long term preservation of this fine artwork and has created some deterioration of the parchment. Thus, the pages have been unbound and separated and are now mounted and enclosed between glass plates.

The original is located in the Pierpont Morgan Library of Midtown Manhattan, New York, NY.

The core element of the MacClesfield Psalter (an illumination from which appears in Figure below) is a personal prayer book containing 150 Psalms. The Psalms are decorated with illustrations such as the one shown here depicting a lady receiving advances from a suitor (riding the horse left) while a wildman (right) offers her a choice between gallant love and the animal lust of the wildman.

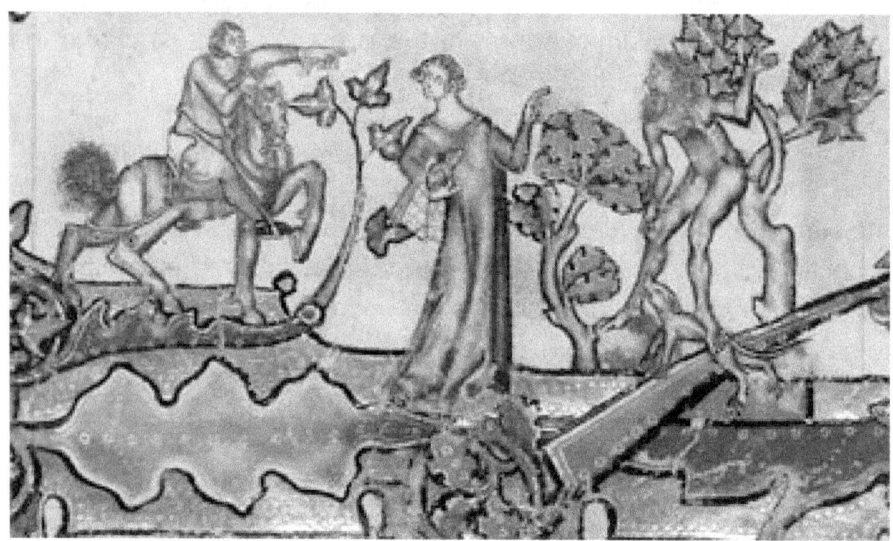

Fig. 13 - *The newly discovered MacClesfield Psalter dates from the 1320s and is considered an an important example of the East Anglian Gothic School. The horseman and a lady with a small dog encounter a wodewose. The subject matter is fairly common and found in many artistic works of the Gothic period and in later artistic eras.*

Discussion

Without photographic technology ancient and classical populations lacked the means by which to "capture the moment" and depict personal encounters they had with bipedal hairy primates and achieve the realism and detail possible today. Still, the painters, sculptors, potters, and craftsmen of the past did manage to leave us a legacy of curious images of BHP "sightings" to follow from their time into ours.

Some of the depictions included in this work are subject to interpretation — others are far more difficult to dismiss as anything other than what they appear to be and is suggested here.

Practicality prevents me from including here all the images that are in my files and those countless others that are undoubtedly available throughout the world in public and private art collections and image repositories.

As this document is only a discussion and not a tome I cannot, in this context, present an extensive scholarly dissertation on each of the example images I have selected with additional support for the attributions that I have offered within these pages. Discussions of this extent will have to wait for future articles on specific items and the controversies that arise about them, or perhaps later updates or an expansion of this document.

Nevertheless, through art we have witnessed a transition, over the span of 50,000 years, wherein BHP creatures have been perceived as akin to us to something quite different. From companion to competition – something familiar to something foreign — as human civilization has moved from the archaic to the advanced.

While the ideas I have expressed within the context of this report will most certainly be subject to continued discussion, and perhaps even ridicule, the reader should recognize that my purpose in conducting this examination is to engender an interest and healthy controversy of the subject matter — not to offer incontrovertible "proof" of the existence of Bigfoot through an examination of creative expression over time.

Certainly, some of the questions that are raised about the circumstances surrounding the creation and inspiration of the art work we have reviewed here open new avenues of investigation to pursue to discover the true import and impact of BHPs in art history.

I encourage others to search artistic archives and resources for additional examples of this genre to further explore the topic of this study and I welcome a civil dialogue on the subject matter with others who are fascinated by it.

Endnotes

1. Marlowe, Scott, 2013, *Bigfoot Enigma,* Pangea press pp. 79- 83.

2. Szukalski, Stanislaw, Undated, *Anthropolitical Motivations,* from a search on *Google,com* resulting in website: http://najmita.150m.com// macimszukalskiowa/yetisyny_ang.htm

3. Magraner, Jordi, 1990, *Oral Statements Concerning Living Unknown Hominids: Analysis, Criticism, and Implications for Language Origins,* Association for Troglodytes, Valance, France, 1990

4. Mayor, Adrienne, 2000, *The First Fossil Hunters: Paleontology in Greek and Roman Times,* Princeton University Press, Princeton, NJ, pp. 100 - 123.

5. Emick, Jennifer, Undated, *Green Man,* appearing in *About: Alternative Religions,* http://altreligion.about.com/library/glossary/symbols/ bldefsgreenman.htm.

6. Pounds, Norman John Greville, 2000, *A History of the English Parish: The Culture of Religion from Augustine to Victoria,* Cambridge University Press, Cambridge, England, p.357.

7. Vaux, J. H. (1989), 32. The Canterbury Monsters. Gillingham: Meresborough.

8. Toman, Rolf (1996), 341. Die Kunst der Romanik: Architektur - Skulptur - Malerei. Köln

9. Briggs, Katharine (1978). Encyclopedia of Fairies: Hobgoblins, Brownies, Bogies, & Other Supernatural Creatures, Pantheon Fairy Tale and Folklore Library

10. Bony, Jean (1983). French Gothic Architecture of the 12th and 13th Centuries, Berkeley: University of California Press

11. Ernest Hans Gombrich (1995). The Story of the Art, Ed. 16. New York: Phaidon Press.

12. Snyder, James (1989). Medieval Art: Painting, Sculpture, Architecture — 4th-14th Century. New York: Abrams.

13. Moser, Stephanie (1998). Ancestral Images: The Iconography of Human Origins, Cornell University Press

14. Ibid

15. ibid

16. Simonds, Peggy Muñoz (1992) Myth, Emblem, and Music in Shakespeare's Cymbeline: An Iconographic Reconstruction, University of Delaware Press

Bibliography

Davies, Denny, Hofrichter, Jacobs, Roberts and Simon, 2004, *Janson's History of Art: The Western Tradition*, Seventh Edition, Volume 1 & 2, Pearson-Prentice Hall, Saddle River, NJ.

Nigg, Joseph, 1999, *The Book of Fabulous Beasts*, Oxford University Press, New York, NY & Oxford, England.

Mayor, Adrienne, 2000, *The First Fossil Hunters: Paleontology in Greek and Roman Times*, Princeton University Press, Princeton, NJ.

Bayanov, Dmitri and Bourtsev, Igor, June 1976, *On Neanderthal vs. Paranthropus,* appearing in *Current Anthroplogy*, Vol. 17, No. 2

McDermott, W.C. 1938, *The Ape in Antiquity*, The Johns Hopkins Press, Baltimore, MD.

Montagu, M.F. Ashley, Jul., 1940, *Knowledge of the Ape in Antiquity*, appearing in *Isis*, University of Chicago Press, Vol. 32, No. 1., pp. 87-102.

Credits

The author would like to acknowledge the following people and organizations for providing assistance, directly or indirectly, in preparing this work:
'

Corey Chimko
Digital Resources Coordinator
University Photography
Cornell University
Ithaca, NY

Loren Coleman
Director
International Cryptozoology Museum
Portland, ME

The Image Gallery
University of California
San Diego, CA

Gregory Jeemen
Assistant Curator of Old Master Prints
National Gallery of Art
Washington, DC

Adrienne Mayor
Author/ Stanford Univerdity Fellow
Palo Alto CA

Kathy Moskowitz-Strain
Anthropologist
Alliance of Independent Bigfoot Researchers
Sonora, CA

Biographical Names

Index

About the Author

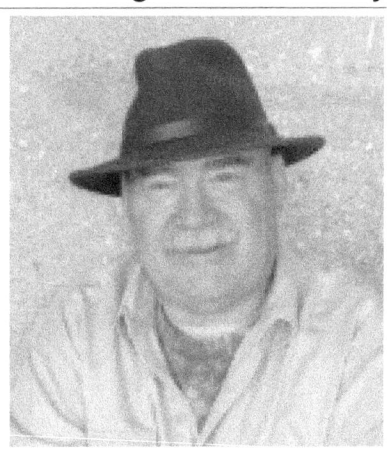

Proclaimed as, "America's most credible cryptozoologist," Scott Marlowe, spends as much time in camos and boots as he does in a Lab coat and oxfords.

A Fellow 0f the famed Pangea Institute and educational consultant to The American Primate Conservation Alliance, Marlowe is the first expert in the field to succeed in establishing an on-going college course in cryptozoology at a state institution of higher learning anywhere in the world.

His cryptozoology course, hailed as one of the "Top Ten" news stories of 2004 by The Cryptozoologist, a well-known insider eMagazine, has won both accolades and awards for its fresh approach and application of forensic science methodologies to the study of enigmatic animals.

Author of "Cryptid Creatures of Florida," (published by CFZ Press of Great Britain) Marlowe "literally wrote the book" on Cryptozoology in the Sunshine State. HIs new book "Bigfoot Enigma" is excitr5ing readers in the Bigfoot community and making skeptics take a second look at "The Big Hairy Guy" with a fresh perspective.

Marlowe's television credits include, MonsterQuest, Is it True Legend Hunters, Destination Truth, Weird Florida, Weird Travels, and William Shatner's Weird or What in addition to countless radio appearances, TV guest spots and lecture tours.